HOW TO BEAT PANDEMIC FATIGUE

Master Your Emotions Of Prolonged Uncertainty Caused By A Pandemic, Included: Lack Of Motivation, Changes In Eating Or Sleeping Habits, Irritability-Stress And Difficulty Concentrating.

By,

Williams Mc Covey

TABLE OF CONTENTS

- From a Declaration of Principles which was accepted and approved equally by a Committee of the American Bar Association and a Committee of Publishers and Associations.

The information provided herein is stated to be truthful and consistent, in that any liability, in terms of inattention or otherwise, by any usage or abuse of any policies, processes, or directions contained within is the solitary and utter responsibility of the recipient reader. Under no circumstances will any legal responsibility or blame be held against the publisher for any reparation, damages, or monetary loss due to the information herein, either directly or indirectly.

Respective authors own all copyrights not held by the publisher.

The information herein is offered for informational purposes solely, and is universal as so. The presentation of the information is without contract or any type of guarantee assurance.

The trademarks that are used are without any consent, and the publication of the trademark is without permission or backing by the trademark owner. All trademarks and brands within this book are for clarifying purposes only and are the owned by the owners themselves, not affiliated with this document.

INTRODUCTION

A new strain of the pandemic virus is concerned with the World Health Organization (WHO) and all international medical personnel. It is known as a pandemic virus, or more commonly as the Wuhan virus, named from the city of Wuhan, China, the epicenter of the virus.

On January 30, 2020, the World Health Organization (WHO) stated that the outbreak should be treated as a global public health emergency. The United States Department of State has issued a maximum alert and asks not to travel to China for the pandemic virus.

Considering the fact that it was first diagnosed in Wuhan, China last year in December, the outbreak of the virushas impacted many other countries, some of which are the United States, and has made a large number of people sick.

So far, the number increases by the day, and it is quite difficult to keep track as hundreds, even thousands, have been either infected or died from the infection while several cases have been detected by the rest of the world outside of China.

Yes, this sounds bad. But before you panic, there are a couple of things you should know. While the virus can prove deadly, it is relatively rare for that to happen, and there be easy prevention methods that you can follow to keep under the risk of contracting the new virus.

In this book, we have gathered information from credible resources about this virus and everything you need to know about it to keep you and loved ones safe and secure.

Let's get started. Shall we?

CHAPTER 1 –WHAT IS PANDEMIC FATIGUE?

What is PANDEMIC FATIGUE?

"Pandemic fatigue" can happen when individuals become exhausted from the pandemic measures and become more reluctant to follow general health practices or just start to silence those messages. A characteristic feeling of burnout can occur since we've needed to adhere to these general health measures for quite a long time now. You may even notify yourself to avoid associating with others or actual signs, such as changes in eating and sleep abilities.

Pandemic fatigue might be experienced more by youth whose groups of friends are not characterized, associating to build relationships and emotional connections significantly in this phase of their life. So, unlike their groups or adult relations who

12

might favor staying in their close group of friends, adults might be enticed to challenge the guidelines as they see their danger to perceive COVID-19 harm to be low.

How does that affect several aspects of life?

Social distancing has increased social isolation and solitude for some individuals, particularly among older adults and individuals who live alone. We are considered social animals. So social disconnection can be very annoying. Furthermore, it can cause a variety of chronic weakness issues, including hypertension and loss of sleep. Individuals had the option to stop meeting with friends in the beginning and stay away from parties. In any case, it tends to be truly difficult to stick the long term with conduct and behavior that can feel like it's all disadvantage and has no potential gain. Try to offset Social distancing with social connectedness. Scientists realize that thinking back or having nostalgia about drinking or smoking is a significant danger for relapse.

What experts say about pandemic fatigue?

Covid fears had people either asking for daily life necessities or running through stores as quickly as possible under the circumstances, avoiding everybody. When they get home, clients cleaned down their goods, vivaciously wash hands, possibly washed up, and changed them into clean clothes. Individuals are bound to remain at home.

Today, there's still no fix or vaccine for the Covid, and diseased numbers are on the rise. Just about a fourth of 1,000,000 Americans are dead of Covid-19, and the danger of disease remains. This is the ideal opportunity to reinforce your purpose and re-dedicate yourself towards precautionary measures.

As a general health care specialist who researches health practices, I know a few mental purposes behind why fatigue sets in. Fortunately, the research proposes a few strategies to help you remain protected just as ensure your mental health and prosperity.

What aspects are affected in our life?

The pandemic fatigue has taken us on fight and flight mode.

It has very serious impacts on our mental and physical health.

You may feel Anxiety, sadness, or depression because of the same old routine of staying home and not meeting your loved ones.

This can also affect the sleep patterns of even a healthy person.

What to do to BEAT THE PANDEMIC FATIGUE?

Take time out for yourself. Try to think positive and do all the precautionary measures necessary for covid avoidance.

There are a few things that can make you strong during this covid fatigue.

- Breathing exercises and meditation can help.
- Observe your social media: Stop 'room scrolling' and restrict time on your screens.
- Restore and replenish your energy.
- Be active; do your favorite activity.
- Reflect and Accept.
- Constructive thinking

Pandemic Causes Prolonged Uncertainties in Our Lives, HOW?

Nothing in life remains the same. There is always room for change to help grow and become the best possible versions of ourselves. Steadfastness and determination are key to becoming what we are striving for. There may come vicissitudes, highs, and lows, and these lows and highs of life shape us into the person we aim to become, and one must not fear them. Uncertainty in life is something that we should not fear; it comes naturally and is unavoidable.

With uncertainty in our lives, we can take up challenges and risks, which eventually leads us out of our comfort zone. Getting out of our comfort zone means we are ready to seek more opportunities and fortunes. Uncertainty plays an important role in our lives, which we cannot understand or comprehend right now but would eventually do.

While some people like the concept and the role that the uncertainty elements play in their lives, others are not much comfortable with its idea. Also, as life is not always smooth and steady, sometimes it is a bumpy ride where one is unsure what would happen next. Uncertainty has grown and crawled into our lives nowadays like never before. Due to the current pandemic situation where life has come to a halt, where the stars and constellations have always envied the hustle-bustle of life on earth now has given it an evil eye. The entire world has been locked inside their houses in an eggshell people call quarantine.

In this situation, we are certain of nothing: economy, finances, physical health, mental health, job, relationships, loved ones, and whatsoever. The life outside our houses is so insecure. You never know who is infected or maybe carrying the virus, what could be the possible carrier of the Covid-19, and what havoc it can cause inside our houses. The precariousness of the fact that we can still keep our jobs or get fired has heightened because the world is going through a huge economic crisis. Millions of people have lost their jobs, and Covid-19 has cost them their livelihood and wellbeing. In a world where a person is not even sure if he will have the job over a specific course of time or not, anxiousness and uncertainty would exist, and that would be completely natural.

The physical health of millions and millions of people has also been compromised due to the widespread of Covid-19. Many of our loved ones have suffered at the hands of this pandemic, hospitals all over the world are crowded with patients, and the health care workers have been working day in, day out to bring down everything under control, yet they can't seem to succeed completely. No vaccine has yet been discovered to treat the Covid-19. In such trying and hard times where everything is so unpredictable, mental health has also been compromised a lot and has started taking its toll and deteriorating physical health. The world has been under lockdown for months, and now again, the lockdown has been imposed as the second wave of the novel Corona Virus is on the rise. The isolation has drained people of energy and compelled them to shun all sorts of human contact.

This pandemic has been harsh not only on the people belonging to the lower class, who do not have access to the necessities of life but also on the middle class and the upper class. Businesses have been shut down. People from all walks of life have been victims of this disease. Just because this pandemic has made everything so uncertain, it has also provoked stress and mental pressure in the masses.

Due to the reasons that have been stated above, it is safe to be concluded that pandemics cause uncertainty over a prolonged period in our lives and will surely leave scars behind that would take a long to heal. But they say that it has become a lifestyle now, so we get to live with it because even after all these months, which have now turned into a year, Covid-19 isn't going anywhere but right here lingering around.

THINGS THAT ARE NOT THE SAME AFTER PANDEMIC:

Our lives have been drastically affected by the spread of coronavirus, and there is no going back. Covid-19 has been a tough test for the world. Never before have the people been affected at this pace and this speed as that of the Covid-19. The lives we led before the outbreak are not the same anymore. They will never be the same because this is now the new normal, and we have to live with this. We have to adapt to this new lifestyle as we cannot turn back time and go back to

Corona free days where there lingered no fear and restlessness, where life was not so uncertain.

Due to the lockdowns imposed worldwide, access to physical education at educational institutes has been greatly affected. The schools, colleges, and universities have been shut down for months, and the education sector has suffered greatly. The students no longer have access to the education they would receive when in their classrooms rather than online education. Third world countries that lack access to technology and the hang of using these technical devices have come to blows.

Not just education but tourism all over the world is also sparring. All the scenic and exotic locations that were the go-to places for the tourists are now seen deserted with no man's sight. Tourism has been affected, as the tourists no longer feel safe when they travel to quench their thirst for discovering picturesque spots worldwide. Besides, flight schedules to the bus and train schedules all have been disrupted.

Work from home is a concept new to many people, going and working in the offices is getting obsolete as work from home is now a new way of working. Many businesses and corporate sectors have encouraged their employees to work from home so they remain safe and keep their families safe from the potential threat of the Covid-19. Work from home may sound appealing to some people because nothing can match the feel of working from their home's comfortable environment. While others may not find it engaging because they tend to work productively in an office environment.

The efficient use of masks is also something which we need to get the hang of. Leaving the house without a mask is also a common practice after the Corona Virus outbreak.

Social distancing is another new concept introduced due to the Covid-19 situation. Maintaining a distance from other people can help slow the spread of the virus. It is practiced all over the world now. To ensure that the public maintains a safe distance from one another, spots have been marked at grocery stores and other public places. Before Covid-19, social distancing was not commonly practiced or known of.

Communication with friends and family has been affected a lot as well, get-togethers with friends had been something which everybody enjoyed and had fun while doing so but now we see our friends every once in a while. Just because everyone is confined to their houses and do not see each other so often has distanced from the relationships we care about. Hanging out with friends or having fun outside with family is not the same anymore. One of the most heartbreaking and saddening changes that the Covid-19 has brought into our lives.

The mental health of many people has been deteriorated because of the rapid spread in the Covid-19, the panic and restlessness that came along with the spread and the fear that it instilled into the masses is also another agonizing change that this pandemic has welcomed into our lives, which is not really welcome.

The life that we spent before the spread of this disease and before the World Health Organization gave it the status of a pandemic after affecting the lives of billions of people in all the world's continents were carefree and easy compared to how it looks like right now. Before the pandemic, we took so many things for granted, so many moments that we would forget to appreciate. All it took was for us to go through a pandemic to appreciate what we had in our lives. Gratitude and appreciation is a virtue we need to incorporate in our lives, so we do not take the good moments in our lives for granted but make the most out of it. Even now going through the pandemic, all we need to do is count our blessings, live one day at a time and fight back courageously no matter what life throws at us. They say when life gives you lemons; make a lemonade.

WHY IS IT IMPORTANT TO OVERCOME THE PROLONGED UNCERTAINTY CAUSED BY A PANDEMIC?

Uncertainty nowadays is more than ever in our lives, where for some people, it allows them to take up risks and challenges. For some, it is a challenge itself that they get to tackle.

Prolonged uncertainty that has been caused by the Covid-19 and other such pandemics have disrupted the life of a common person on so many fronts. Prolonged uncertainty makes a person insecure and constantly makes them feel unsafe in an environment. The day-to-day tasks and activities are compromised and have made people pessimistic where their every approach towards life has become cynical. Everyday life suffers, their relationships with their loved ones suffer, work, finances, etc., everything becomes gloomy. As a result, one feels like burying in a pit from which there seems no escape.

Now that Covid-19 is here to stay, and we get to live with this for how long, that no one knows. It completely depends on how we tackle and deal with the situation and uncertainty as a result of it. It is super important to overcome uncertainty in life because of the havoc it can cause. If a person cannot overcome uncertainty, he would not be able to get comfortable in his or her own skin and life. The person would constantly criticize himself and not accept the imperfections of life because life does not always have to be perfect. There would be times when a person would not know what to do next? There would be randomness all around with surety of not even a thing. Overcoming uncertainty is also important as to not lose focus of life, stay focused and pivoted a person would know what to do next in their life and differentiate between the right and wrong, which would lead them to make the best decision for themselves. Conquering the demon of uncertainty is as important as staying positive in every situation no matter what it is? If a person is unable to overcome uncertainty, he would have a negative approach towards everything, be it the smallest thing in life, there would be no hope and yearning and rather to remain optimistic he would remain more pessimistic towards the issues he is facing with the uncertainty and randomness in his life.

Overcoming uncertainty and especially prolonged uncertainty is important so a person can trust his gut instincts. There would be no doubt and insecurity with whatever they think is right and suitable for any situation. If a person defeats prolonged uncertainty, he would see the bigger picture and have multiple options and not just completely dwell on one solution to whatever problem he comes across. He would always have a contingency plan to rely on if the actual plan is not working out as planned. The contingency plan by a person who is sure about whatever he does would be as strong and reliable as the original main plan.

Letting go is another concept, which we can learn when we can overcome uncertainty.

This way, we do not have to cling to the past but will be open to risks and challenges, and we will eventually become what we aim to become as a person. Letting go would give us a sense of being strong and make us able to achieve whatever we wish for. It would enable us to do something that we have not really done before.

Identifying our uncertainty triggers would prove to be greatly beneficial in overcoming prolonged uncertainty as it is also said that uncertainty is self-generated. Overcoming self-generated and prolonged uncertainty would pave the way towards our growth as a person.

Prolonged uncertainty can make a person a procrastinator. A person would constantly procrastinate and keep delaying whatever is supposed to be done and would not meet deadlines. It is super important for a person to be able to overcome uncertainty in life.

That way, they would keep their schedules up to date, and no work would lag behind. Everything would get completed in time and with due consideration.

With the fear of uncertainty lurking on the head, a person would not actively deal with his emotions. He would keep ignoring them and keep bottling them inside him. Suppressing emotions is one of the most dangerous things a person can do to himself. Doing so would make a person more anxious and depressed. Overcoming uncertainty up to a certain aspect where a person can actively deal with whatever he feels is really essential and important.

Uncertainty is a natural part of life and somewhat unavoidable too. It is totally upon us how we overcome it so we can become a great person, we get to deal with uncertainty daily, and as some people fear it, others like to take it as a challenge and deal with it.

Fearing uncertainty is not what is desirable but what's important is to overcome the uncertainty of life. Life is full of surprises. Nothing in life ever remains the same; one day is different from the other. Every day brings us new challenges and new opportunities. Life is not a roses bed, but it is a bumpy roller coaster ride with its own ups and downs. In conditions like such, how we are facing nowadays, it is really important to overcome uncertainty because it would not ease anything but would keep adding to the stress and, in turn, keep us more anxious. The whole world is in the middle of a pandemic right now, with its cases increasing every second and people dying all over the world. It is very difficult to overcome uncertainty. Another thing that can ease up the stress and help us reduce uncertainty is to accept it and then learn to cope with it.

The first step to coping up with uncertainty is accepting it if a person cannot accept it and has a hard time accepting it. Then it would become difficult to cope up with. Dealing with uncertainty or uncertain conditions begins with having trust and a strong belief in our selves. No matter what happens, this belief and trust shall always be there. There is no room for self-doubt and being self-critical. One shall always be kind to themselves whenever going through such hard and trying times. Being harsh on oneself would do nothing but cause more damage and harm to the mental health affecting it even more.

Reflecting on past experiences, the good and positive aspects also greatly help in dealing with uncertainty. Times may not always be hard, and whatever good the past times brought into our lives shall be cherished. Learning from mistakes is eminent, and whatever mistakes have been made rather than being self-critical, lessons could be learned from those mistakes, so they are not repeated.

Taking an interest in a new skill or learning a new sport also proves to be helpful when dealing with uncertainty. Learning a new skill helps in boosting confidence and lets us step out of our comfort zone. Once we are out of our comfort zone, dealing with uncertain conditions becomes relatively easy.

Stressing upon the things that are out of our control and dwelling in those things, which we cannot seem to sway. Stressing on those things can only add to the anxiety and depression in such trying times when the pandemic is upon us unleashing horrors.

Another factor, which greatly helps in dealing with uncertainty, is taking advice and help from the people we trust. Help from the people we trust will be something that would benefit us. Rather than isolating and keeping everything to ourselves, all the negative thoughts would only damage us.

Uncertainty needs to be addressed with bravery, right in its face. Stay strong no matter what because, as we have already discussed earlier, it is nothing but unavoidable and natural. It would always exist lurking around our wellbeing. It depends upon us only on how we deal with it. It is our battle with the demons and the bravery we fought this fight with. After going through all this, surviving in the most uncertain of the conditions with this pandemic of Covid-19, one would realize how strong and resilient he is. Pandemic is not going away anywhere, and so is the uncertainty of life. It is important to accept it, deal with it, and learn ways to overcome it. I cannot stress enough that the key to success here is not to be harsh on oneself but to accept and learn how to live with it, keeping in mind to stay clear-headed ourselves and keep others around us sane. In such hard times, all we need is the unending support of each other.

What if you fail to overcome uncertainties during a pandemic?

Uncertainty is normal nowadays. The current COVID-19 pandemic has increased uncertainty over the economy, business, accounts, connections, and obviously, physical and emotional well-being. However, as individuals, we crave security. We need to have a feeling of authority over our lives and prosperity. Fear and uncertainty can leave you stressed and weak over different aspects of your life. It can exhaust you emotionally.

We all know how much uncertainty we can endure throughout life. A few people face challenges and carry on with unusual lives, while others find life extremely upsetting. If you feel defeated by vulnerability and stress, realize that you are in good company; many of us are in the same situation right now. It is vital to understand that regardless of how vulnerable and miserable you feel, you can take steps to manage natural conditions, reduce your anxiety, and face the trouble with more confidence.

Think how to adapt to uncertainty

While we may not recognize it, uncertainty is a characteristic and unavoidable part of life. To know about our lives that are steady or certain, and keeping in mind that we have authority over many things, we cannot control all the things that happen to us. As the Covid pandemic has appeared, life can change rapidly and unusually. You may have become weakened, lost your employment, or ended up battling to put food on the table or keep your family protected. You might be emotional about when the pandemic will end or if life will get back to business as usual.

To adapt to this vulnerability, many of us focus on predicting the future and avoiding disturbing happenings. Stressing can cause it to seem like you have some power over uncertain conditions. You may accept that it will help you find an answer for your issues or set you up for being dreadful. Perhaps if you obsess about an issue long enough, consider every chance, or read all feelings, you will find an answer and have the option to control the result. Consistent stressing cannot give you power over bad occasions; it just dismisses your pleasure in the present, drains your energy, and keeps you up all night. In any case, there are more beneficial approaches to adapt to vulnerability—and that starts with changing your mentality.

The accompanying tips can push you to:

- focus on controlling those things that are profoundly influencing you
- Challenge your requirement for support.
- Figure out how to endure, even understand, the unavoidable vulnerability of life.
- Reduce your uneasiness and feelings of anxiety.

Tip 1: Take actions over the things you can control

life is unsure right now—and numerous things stay away from your control. However, you cannot control the spread of an infection, the recovery of the economy, or whether you will have a check one week from now, you are not weak. Whatever your beliefs or individual conditions, rather than stressing over the current circumstances, try to pull together your mind to make a move over the perspectives in your control.

For instance, if you have lost your employment or pay during this troublesome time, you have power over how much energy you put into looking for online work, sending resumes, or systems administration with your contacts. Essentially, if you are stressed over your well-being during the Covid pandemic, you can make a move by consistently washing your hands, cleaning surfaces, avoiding crowds, and looking out for weak friends and neighbors. By focusing on an issue that you can control along these lines, you will change from ineffective stressing and start thinking into dynamic critical thinking. All conditions are unique, and you may find that everything you can control is your mentality and impulsive reaction in certain circumstances.

Effectively manage your feelings.

When conditions are out of your control, it is anything but difficult to get overpowered by fear and negative feelings. You may believe that controlling how you feel, trying to act courageously, or driving yourself to be goodwill give the best result. However, rejecting or extinguishing your feelings will just expand stress and uneasiness and make you more powerless against despair or burnout. When you cannot do anything else about a circumstance, you can effectively face up to your feelings—even the most negative and terrible ones. Allowing yourself to face uncertainty in this manner can help you with decreasing stress, better deal with your conditions, and find a feeling of peace as you manage difficulties.

Tip 2: Challenge your desires for certainty

While uncertainty and change are inevitable parts of life, we in our lives are adaptable to the consequences they bring to our life. Stress over every imaginable situation, you may:

- Irrationally look for consolation from others. You over and again inquire as you are making the correct choice, review the social media, or search out the direction with an end goal to eliminate vulnerability from your life.

- Micromanage individuals. You will not select projects for other people, either at the office or home. You may even attempt to drive individuals around you to change, to make their conduct predictable for you.

- Procrastinate. By delaying your decisions, you plan to maintain a strategic distance from the vulnerability that follows. You will learn approaches to defer or delay simulation—or even avoid certain circumstances altogether—trying to keep unfortunate things from happening.

- Over and again, check things. You call or text your family, companions, or children over and over to ensure they are protected. You browse and re-browse messages before sending, twofold check records to guarantee you have not missed whatever could affect the flexibility of things to come.

Instructions to challenge these manners

You can challenge the behaviors you have received to lighten the difficulty of vulnerability by asking yourself the following questions:

What are the benefits of certainty? What are the limitations?

Life can change in a second, and it is loaded up with startling occasions and amazements—however, that is not a terrible thing. For each frightful happening, for example, a car crash or genuine clinical determination, there are beneficial things that occur out of nowhere too—a fantasy bid for employment, an unexpected compensation rise, or an unexpected call from an old companion. Opportunity frequently emerges from the unexpected, and confronting uncertainty in life can likewise help you figure out how to adjust, reverse difficulties, and increase your flexibility. It can assist you with developing personally.

How much can you be certain about life?

Does anybody have employment forever, assurance of good health, or complete certainty over what tomorrow will bring? Manners, for example, stressing, micromanaging, and lingering, offer the illusion of having some command over a situation, yet what do they change in reality? The fact of the matter is regardless of the time you try to create and plan for each likely result, and life will find a method of surprising you. All making progress toward hope truly does is fuel stress and tension.

Do you accept terrible things will happen because a result is uncertain? What is the probability they will?

At the point when you are faced with uncertainty, it is anything but difficult to overestimate the probability of something awful occurring—and lower your capacity to adapt if it does. In any case, given that the probability of something awful happening is low, even at this problematic time, is it credible to live with that little possibility and spotlight rather on the almost certain results? Ask your loved ones how they adapt to vulnerability in specific conditions. could you do what they would recommend?

By testing your support demand, you can start to abandon negative practices, reduce pressure and stress, and save time and energy for more viable purposes.

Tip 3: Learn to acknowledge uncertainty

Regardless of the amount, you try to take out uncertainty and instability from your life; you, as of now, acknowledge uncertainty consistently. Each time you go across a road, get in the driver's seat of a car, or eat takeaways or café food, you are permitting a degree of uncertainty. You believe that the traffic will stop, you will not have a mishap, and all you are eating is protected. The odds of something terrible occurring in these conditions is little, so you acknowledge the danger and proceed onward without requiring certainty. In case you are strict, you likely acknowledge some uncertainty and vulnerability as a feature of your confidence.

At the point when extreme feelings of fear and stress grab hold, it may be difficult to think intelligently and precisely weigh up the likelihood of something terrible happening. To help you with getting more open-minded and tolerating uncertainty, the accompanying suggestions can help:

- Distinguish your uncertainty triggers. Uncertainty will, in general, act naturally produced, through extreme stressing or a critical viewpoint, for instance. some uncertainty can be created by outer sources, particularly on occasions such as this. Studying media stories that respect most pessimistic scenario situations, investing energy in online media in gossipy tidbits and misleading statements, or essentially speaking with emotional companions would all be able to fuel your feelings of fear and vulnerabilities. By understanding your triggers, you can move to stay away from or decrease your presentation to them.

Notice when you feel the demand for certainty. Notice when you begin to feel restless and frightful about a circumstance, start to stress over what-uncertainties, or feel like a circumstance is far more unfortunate than it is. Search for the actual signs that you are feeling emotional. You may see the strain in your neck or shoulders, shortness of breath, the beginning of a migraine, or emptiness in your stomach. Rest for a minute to stop and look that you're longing for comfort or certainty.

Allow yourself to feel the vulnerability. Rather than participating in worthless attempts to oversee the uncertainty, let yourself experience the uneasiness of vulnerability. Like all feelings, if you permit yourself to feel fear and vulnerability, they will pass anyway. Focus on the current moment and your breathing, and permit yourself to feel and notice the vulnerability you are facing. Take some easy, deep breaths or try a plan to keep you in the present.

CHAPTER 2 – HOW TO MASTER YOUR EMOTIONS OF PROLONGED UNCERTAINTY CAUSED BY A PANDEMIC?

Many changes have gone with the COVID-19 pandemic. Everyday plans have been interrupted; numerous people have been detached from loved ones, and tensions are high. Each individual responds diversely to troublesome or distressing events. While feeling stressed is typical and normal during a common disaster, it is anything but difficult to fall into excitement or feeling overpowered. If you do not appreciate yourself, many awkward feelings can emerge, for example, resentment, insult, disappointment, and misery. Unaddressed emotional concerns can prompt negative results, for example, changes with sleep and hunger, trouble thinking, sicknesses, stressed relationships, and even thoughts of suicide. Making time to think about yourself during this season of vulnerability is significant for emotional prosperity so you can think clearly and help your drawn-out health and satisfaction.

Here are a few different ways to think about yourself privately, given the stress of living at home and socially separating from loved ones.

Self-Care Strategies

1. Do a daily practice

if you cannot adhere to your ordinary daily schedule, you can make another one describes staying indoors, telecommuting, or another day by day exercises that had to change. Doing a daily practice or a custom can help make "another ordinary" by completing some structure every day. Distinguish what you appreciate doing practically consistently and put aside time every morning or night to finish those exercises. Maybe you get up fifteen minutes ahead of schedule so you can make the most of your espresso in bed. Perhaps you start each day by making your bed, followed by some light extending and an energetic walk outside. Incorporate old and new helpful abilities into your new daily schedule.

2. Daily Check-In

Make time to check in with yourself consistently. Notice and acknowledge how you feel. Possibly this is before anything else, in your day, or before bed. Choosing when and how regularly to check in with yourself helps take heat and control in your life. Find a pleasant spot to sit upright and close your eyes. Take a full breath, relax your jaw, and check-in with your mind and your body. Try not to attempt to transform anything; simply notice it, and focus on it. How would you feel? Do you feel tight or tense anyplace? What are you holding? Take a couple of deep breaths. You may see less force if you can sit with your affections for a couple of moments. Feelings exist for an explanation - they let you realize when something feels right or wrong. Disregarding feelings may briefly cause you to feel better; in any case, just recognizing every feeling can help you feel like any negative feelings do not compel you. The other uplifting news about feelings is they are continually developing.

3. Reexamine Your Thoughts

By emphasizing circumstances instead of difficulties and on what you are appreciative of, you can positively reexamine negative thoughts. Possibly you presently have more opportunity to connect with loved ones you do not converse with frequently enough, or perhaps now you can grasp a pastime you never felt like you possessed enough energy for. Further, you can challenge negative or restless thoughts by recording why the idea is causing you to feel how you feel. Question it vigorously. Is your concern sensible? Additionally, recording three things you appreciate every day is a decent token of what is positive in your life. When making an appreciation list, center around the little positives that you may somehow or another ignore.

4. Set aside a few minutes for Rest

Making time to loosen up is basic for powerful self-care. Regularly, an individual can feel frustrated or on edge when choosing to rest. Possibly the clothing should be cleaned, or the dishes are piling up. Nonetheless, it is important to set aside a few minutes for yourself to sit idle or something you appreciate performing for yourself. Planning "down time" or "personal time" is a decent method to rest your brain. Maybe you can read a book, or just sit outside, taking a look at the sky. Possibly you will drink your number one sort of tea while looking out the window. You are simply the best individual to allow to rest, approval of being caring and cherishing with yourself. Deal with yourself like you would treat a friend.

5. Take part in Healthy Activities

Deal with your body - intellectually and genuinely. Take deep breaths frequently. Get seven to eight hours of relaxing sleep every night by restricting TV, phone, and PC use preceding heading off to the room. Cutoff daytime naps to no longer than 20 minutes. Likewise, it remains active day by day. Eat a regular eating routine and drink enough water to remain hydrated. Every one of these exercises can help you improve your sleep around night time, which can help you feel rested toward the start of the day. A very much refreshed brain is a quiet mind.

6. Remain Connected to Friends and Family

Particularly during emergency or trouble times, we as people flourish with social corporations and connectedness. At the point when you are not ready to drop by a companion's home or have grandkids come to visit, you may turn out to be sad and tragic. A way to fight this is to set up scheduled calls, Zoom meetings, or FaceTime recordings with loved ones to keep up a feeling of connectedness. Booking routine calls can support you and your friends and family during periods of stress. It is essential to discuss your feelings, just as appreciate the unnecessary discussion of the pandemic.

For adapting to these issues, we stress 'trauma-informed " methods:

- Use techniques to lessen pressure for the day, including connections that help a clever attitude (extremist acknowledgment, self-sympathy, positive test examinations), just as mind-body methods that reduce pressure responses, for example, breathing activities, meditation, exercises (with social distancing), and social help.

- Understand and reduce terrible responses. It is essential to support patients, suppliers, and staff has a sense of security. Empowering, the early looking for care is essential.

- Comprehend hierarchical and community points of view. It is useful to understand that arrangements must be public and not simply singular in light of large failures and terrible accidents (like one-on-one treatment). As confirmed by Jack Saul, Ph.D., a mutual point of view gives sources; for example, communal perspective upholds companies, systems, performance connections, and safe conditions. Trauma-informed practices and principles help cause people to feel safe and hence more managed. It incorporates organizing connections (as social help and association can cradle pressure reactions), making actual security (a protected climate reduces the pressure reaction and guarantees normal reasoning, judgment, and attentional control can happen), and emotional wellbeing (to help staff comprehend what is in store).

Tips for everybody

- **Remain protected from the infection**

For this situation, the greatest healthy practices (physical removal and handwashing) that decrease the COVID-19 infection transmission are necessary for stress administration. Stay at home when you can. When outside the home, wash your hands completely and habitually.

To support us with making the thorough hand-washing another ability, try this: "Wash as though you just chopped up a jalapeno pepper (without gloves), and you currently need to place it in your contact eye lens." Do not fail to remember the sides of every single finger, the back of hands, palms, the ridges and nail beds, and the back of nails. Wash for at least 20 seconds - as long as it takes you to quietly murmur the Alphabet Song, Happy Birthday, or present the Loving Kindness

Prayer. If you are a quick hummer, state it twice.

- **Limit media to decrease stress**

At this point, you have heard this suggestion ordinarily, and there is research behind it: Watching or looking through the media makes us considerably more emotional An excess of information and visual pictures about a horrible accident can make signs of post-awful stress issues and chronic weakness years after the fact, as per research by UC Irvine's Roxy Silver, Ph.D., and others.

Try to restrict COVID-19 media presentation to close to two times every day (e.g., checking for refreshes in the first part of the day and before supper) and attempt to try not to find out about COVID-19 preceding sleep time. Take a pledge not to convey (and in this way cause) dreadful stories to loved ones. The media regularly makes a distorted impression of worldwide excitement.

- **Get and give warm, soothing social assistance by video, telephone, or text.**

This is basic! Setting aside some effort to share your thoughts and to listen and support others will go far. Talking with other people who have our future benefits on a fundamental level causes us to feel safe. Use telephone, video, text, or email. Luckily these new highways of social contact are limitless assets. Something other than offering social help about the current emergency is a smart thought to use these relationships with to talk about the things you frequently would - have your book club on the network, for instance - which can make connectedness emotions. Host a supper using FaceTime or Zoom so you can talk while you eat (and talk about some sure things, not simply this emergency). Adoring and thinking about our pets can be a remarkable stress reliever for us as well!

"Social Distancing" is essential; it is physical separating while we try to remain socially associated. We should change to that thought!

Lack of motivation during the pandemic situation. How to motivate yourself?

The COVID-19 pandemic is a shock to every one of us—and that can appear to be desensitizing on some events. However, it is an ideal opportunity to make essential steps to help you gain inspiration in your own and professional life. To many, it's a terrible, boring adaptation of Groundhog Day … and the laws are evolving day by day. It's normal for such chaotic circumstances to cause physical and mental lethargy.

1. **Fear**. Some of the diverse inquiries COVID has set off:

- Temporarily: How will this influence my profession and accounts? When will this be finished? When would I be able to see my loved ones? Will I become ill? What will life become once the lockdown is lifted? The suggestions and questions are endless. On top of reducing normalcy for everything easy and comfortable, economical and health worries are causing tremendous stress and self-confidence.

- In the long term: Will this be happening again? How might I be ready later on? What would I be able to get from this?

2. **Isolation.** The security in place phenomenon has influenced a range of difficulties. For many, being separated from co-workers, friends, and family members is away from stress, contrary to being satisfied as a human being. While it has connected families and created a different opportunity to eventually slow down and smell the flowers, for others, it's claustrophobic, with little private space. Technology has improved society with the impression, somewhat bridging the gap and telling us that "we are all together in this." Still, social media can give an escape from the stress—pushing down personal or professional responsibilities.

3. **Lack of focus.** News headlines, changing by the hour, manage how, when, and where we can lead, talk, and breathe in public. Without being surprised, productivity can fall between the constant confusion and disruption to our daily routine. Letting go of power isn't easy, yet it's an essential skill set

at the minute. It's time to understand what you can put things to control.

Being at the notion of this storm can make you feel weak and detached from every other thing that makes up your health. But if you see, the silver linings, on a micro and macro level. From a personal view, you do have the opportunity to control your life, even if in little ways. Some ideas are:

1. Design a schedule. Having some appearance of a daily schedule will empower you. Fix your plan the night before, remembering it's flexible. At least you'll have an opening point for the following day—and it will help you stay motivated.

2. Separate work from your own life. Working from home is new to many, so discipline is the message of the day. Get up early, dress, get your space designed, and tell yourself that you're finally in control of your waking time.

Avoid the appeal to read the news headlines. Instead, note down your plans for the day as a "starter engine." Do your chores during non-business hours. You need structure and control—which will encourage greater action.

3. Exercise and walk outdoors. Get yourself in action. You don't require to set up a difficult routine for the latest YouTube exercise trend. Beginning with a 20-minute walk. No stress. Remember the advice of Harry Truman: ***"Imperfect actions are better than perfect inactions."***

4. Learn relaxation methods. There's no lack of meditation apps, and yoga is a great way to free tension from the last COVID news. Think about the strategies that give you peace of mind.

5. Connect. Stay in touch with colleagues and family by phone, video apps, social media, text, email, or all of the above. This may be a suitable opportunity to reach out to those you are trying to contact. Are there colleagues, family, or networking connections with whom you have lost touch? They would enjoy learning from you now.

6. Give time to yourself. Read a book. Learn that recipe, try it, watch TV; paint a picture; listen to your favorite music, or enjoy the comedy film you wanted. Maybe it's time to check on yourself. Just don't put unnecessary stress on yourself to overperform in any field, or you may miss out on relaxation through this change.

7. Eat healthily. It can be simple to eat healthy foods or binge through stressful times but avoid the appeal to eat, drink, or drugs as an avoidance. This could be the opportunity to learn about eating habits, as you have the time now to give to it.

8. Focus. Reduce the usual offenders of distraction. While at home, if others are continually interfering with you, set some rules. Put your Cell phone on Do Not Disturb mode for certain times of the day. Use earbuds. Take time for calls and video calls—plan specific times of the day to review news updates and social media.

9. Check in with your boss and team regularly. be assure that you are in contact with your supervisor and/or clients, particularly if you're concerned about the business environment. Your team may require to hear for reassurance, too. Use your emotional intelligence with all points, in and outside the workplace, as their anxiety levels are high. A regular check-in will keep you grounded. If you are unemployed, this is a great time to reach out to your arrangement and continue being there. Set goals weekly for checking in with considered employers as markets reopen.

10. Set goals monthly, three months out, or longer, maybe. The next three months are crucial in what COVID-19 could settle in our lives. But this shouldn't hinder you from moving on with your life.

It is easy to let the thrill of a pandemic consume you or at least slow you down. But every day, you can take real steps to manage your ideas on exactly how you would spend your time.

The pandemic is also expanding our different ways of reasoning and acting in the face of uncertainty. We're always deciding on limited and probably inaccurate information. We never know whether or not we'll get an illness, experience an accident, or be in the wrong position at the wrong moment.

Making decisions and choices about something new can involve the following:

1. Risk. In daily conversations, we talk about risks, not opportunities, but that's technically incorrect. To understand the risk of something, scientists have to know a lot about that. Calculating risk requires a place where potential results can be completely recognized and their expectations associated. That only results under controlled circumstances.

2. Uncertainty is when the standards and scales of issues are known, but their probabilities are not. We might understand a lot about the abuse of feeling isolated. However, our

predictions of how much will affect people during distancing could still be uncertain, as special probabilities remain hard to predict.

3. Uncertainty is when the probability of results being in question. What is a fair length of time to measure for unfavorable health influences of a new COVID-19 medication? What specifically should we include? What should we neglect as unimportant? These are not merely scientific questions. They depend on the preferences and desires, and motivations of the people making the decisions.

4. Ignorance: Maybe we do not even know what we don't know.

All of these relate to our recognition of COVID-19. There is a level of unpredictability, uncertainty, or confusion behind all choices. We make our decision based on one version of the information that we are aware of. The reaction to uncertainty doesn't have to be fearful to make a decision. The COVID-19 pandemic requires fast choices. But it is essential to be as accurate as possible in accepting what we don't know and improving our plans as better knowledge becomes available. Whether on COVID-19 or other important decisions affecting people, there are trade-offs. One strategic approach is another factor that people think polarizes how we think about answers to COVID-19.

How to manage changes in your eating and sleeping etc., daily habits?

The food you eat can influence your wellbeing and your risk for specific ailments. To eat more healthy food, you may need to change your daily routine. You may need to change a few things in your current state. Your current situation includes everything around you, similar to your house or the place you work. You don't have to roll out large changes to eat more healthily. Also, you don't need to change your abilities altogether. It's ideal to set small objectives and change your inclinations a bit at a time. Over the long term, little changes can have a major effect on your health.

This information will help you with rolling out important changes for a healthy diet.

- Changing your dietary patterns and your current situation can assist you with eating more useful nutrients.
- A healthy eating regimen is useful for your general health. It additionally can help you with reaching an ideal weight and maintain it.
- To improve your dietary patterns, it's ideal for making little life changes that

you can continue doing over the long term.

How can you change your eating patterns?

To try an eating regimen, you need to change certain things. Remember that you can change your eating patterns a little at a time. Little changes are easier to make and can cause better health.

Here are a few different ways to change your dietary patterns:

- Eat more natural products, low-fat dairy items (low-fat milk and low-fat yogurt), vegetables, and whole-grain nutrients at home and work—focus on adding healthy food to your eating regimen instead of simply excluding poor nutrients.
- Try to eat a family feast each day at the kitchen or dining table.

- Pack your healthy snacks for work. This lets you have more authority over what you eat.
- Put your snacks on a plate and avoid eating from the whole package. This encourages you to control the amount you eat.
- Try not to skip or postpone suppers, and make certain plans with your friends as well. If you ignore your feelings of appetite, you may end up eating excessively or picking an unhealthy snack. If you regularly feel excessively hungry.
- Eat your dinners with your friends. Relax and make most of your time, and don't eat fast. try to make smart eating a delight, not a job.
- Drink water rather than high-sugar drinks (counting high-sugar juice drinks).

Food is likewise identified with rest by craving and digestion. Examination by Dr. Van Cauter shows that individuals who don't get enough rest have more cravings because their leptin levels (leptin is a hunger managing hormone) fall, causing hunger to increase. This connection between craving and sleep gives additional proof that sleep and obesity are connected. To finish it off, the mental signs of fatigue, sleep, and hunger are comparable. Along these lines, when you're feeling lazy, you may feel like you have to move toward the refrigerator rather than a bed.

Before hitting the sack, it is essential to unplug and prepare yourself for a relaxing night. The primary activity is to bid farewell to all COVID-19-related news. We propose:

- 1-2 hours before bed, disconnect from email, news, and whatever else that makes a brain start thinking and start focusing on being relaxed. Farewell, the COVID-19 news; believe that it will be there toward the beginning of the day.

- Turn off the lights and do things that are relaxing. Relaxing exercises shift by the individual, regularly incorporate reading, listening to music.
- Avoid alcohol before sleep time and end caffeine intake after the evening.
- Keep a regular sleep schedule.

Keep up a regular morning routine.

Suppose credible try to get some sunlight early in the morning. Together, these will help control your circadian rhythm.

Try not to toss around in bed.

If you can't nod off or awaken and can't fall back to sleep, don't toss in bed for more than 15-20 minutes. Get up and finish your pending work, do relaxing exercises until you feel lazy, and then get back to bed.

Make your room a holy place to rest.

Make certain to keep your room dark, calm, and cool.

Mind your day to secure your night

What you do during the day can affect your night. Remote working bears the cost of service, yet also may cause sedentary conduct and napping. Resting can destroy your sleeping patterns, making it harder to nod off around night time. Inactivity can likewise prompt lighter sleep and fewer sentiments following a night's sleep at the beginning of the day.

How to deal with the irritability, stress, and other difficulties?

Irritability is something we all experience; however, what separates it from other emotional states is the degree to which it spoils the emotional environment around us. For sure, irritability is the carbon monoxide of emotional poisons. One individual's bad-tempered state of mind can give pessimism and stress-prompting vibes that negatively affect the whole office, family, or homeroom.

When we feel irritable, we feel anxious, tense, fussy, and vigorous. Our immunity is weak, and we are more prone to be disturbed by the kinds of minor disappointments we normally ignore. Our responses to difficulties are prone to be more powerful than expected, making us snap, bark, and criticize everyone around us. When the manager is angry, word rapidly spreads around the workplace to avoid their direction. When mother or father returns home from work in an irritable state, it takes a couple of moments for the children to exchange recognizing looks and quietly go into their rooms (or put on their headphones).

Irritability is not healthy for the individual facing it. Our stress hormones release, and we enter a similar fight-or-flight pattern our ancestors did when they were on bear-watch duty at the cavern's entrance. The smallest development or disorder can take us a leap and respond as though we face an attack, with nary a risk in sight.

 Many people would cheerfully snap their fingers and free themselves of this harmful intense state if they could. Oh, finger-snapping is anything but a successful treatment. However, there are seven key things you can do to cut yourself down when you're feeling irritable or anxious.

1. Sort out the source.

The ideal approach to lessen irritability is to sort out what's making you irritable—and afterward address it. Recognize when you previously got irritated and consider what may have set you off. It's important to recall that while your responses may feel complex right now, the issue set off them may be basic.

2. Reduce your caffeine and alcohol intake.

An excess of caffeine during the day and a lot of alcohol around evenings are irritability for some individuals. So, consider quitting.

3. It's often the small things

We regularly excuse considering things that shouldn't make us irritable regardless of whether they do. Be straightforward with yourself about annoying you: Simply recognizing that something is making you irritable is regularly enough to bring some relief.

4. Connect with your compassion.

Being empathetic—with yourself—can be an amazing method to quiet your intensive feelings. Recognize (in your mind) that you feel truly irritable—and how unpleasant it is. When imagine getting a hug from somebody who thinks about you and you feel somewhat better, use your empathy to consider how it has caused people around you to feel and that it is necessary not to take it out on them.

5. Gain perspective.

We generally feel annoyed by little things that we won't recall in a coming couple of days or weeks. Take a couple of moments to help yourself remember the bigger picture— the things that are working out positively in your life and the things you can appreciate, for example, health and business. However, if you feel too upset to consider doing this sort of reasoning, go for therapy.

6. Free yourself of negative energy.

Since irritability activates our fight-or-flight reaction sets, it may be a smart thought to go for a speedy walk or run, or, if that is unrealistic, do some fast push-ups or crunches to free yourself of excess energy that may be filling your mind with anxiety. Open-air on a comfortable walk could also do good to you.

7. Get calm or alone time.

Locate a quiet spot to fully consider things or to withdraw from the disturbance and action around you. Irritability can be your brain's method of warning you that you need a break, so you must take one. Listen to some good music, do some stretching or yoga, study, or take a bath. When you're set, take a deep breath and set yourself up to reconnect so your system isn't shocked back into anxiety once you reenter the fight.

Three steps to take when feeling anxious.

1. Acknowledge when it is causing you an issue

Try to make the connection between feeling tired or sick and the weights you are confronted with. Post for actual alerts, for example, tense muscles, over-sleepiness, cerebral pains, or migraines.

2. Recognize the causes

Try to distinguish the hidden causes. Sort the possible explanations behind your stress into three classifications

1) those with a practical solution

2) those that will improve with time

3) those you can't take care of anything

Try to address the concern of those in the second and third parties and let them go.

3. Review your way of life

- Might you be able to be taking on something over the top?
- Are those things you are doing could be given over to another person?
- Would you be able to get things done comfortably?

To follow up on these questions' responses, you may need to organize things you are trying to achieve and re-arrange your life. This will assist with releasing tension that can arise out of trying to do everything simultaneously.

Seven steps to help shield yourself from stress

1. Eat healthily

Eating healthy can lessen the risks of diet-related diseases. Proofs are indicating how food influences our mood and how eating regularly can improve this. You can settle your thoughts of success by guaranteeing that your eating regimen gives sufficient brain supplements, for example, basic nutrients and minerals, just as water.

2. Know about smoking and drinking alcohol

Make an effort not to, or lessen, the sum you smoke and drink alcohol.

Even though they may appear to decrease stress initially, this is misleading as they frequently make issues worse.

3. Exercise

Try to incorporate real exercise into your life as it tends to help relieve stress. Indeed, even going out and getting some open-air, and taking some actual light exercise, such as taking a walk to the shops, can truly help

4.Take break

Set aside an effort to relax. Find some harmony between working for others and commitment to yourself; this can truly lessen anxiety and intense feelings. Talk to yourself that it is alright to organize self-care ·

5. Be careful

Care is a brain-body way to deal with life that encourages us to relate diversely to experiences. It includes focusing on our considerations and feelings such that we build our capacity to manage troublesome situations and settle on savvy decisions.

- Try to practice care consistently
- The care plan can be practiced anywhere, anytime.

Research has recommended that it can decrease the impacts of stress, tension, and related issues, for example, sleep loss, weak focus, and low mind-sets, in some people.

6. Get some peaceful sleep

1. Could your physical or emotional well-being be affecting your capacity to sleep?
2. Would you be able to change your current situation to help improve your sleep?
3. Would you be able to get up in the morning when your mind is stressing around all night?
4. Would you be able to implement little changes to your way of life to support your peaceful sleep?

7. Try not to be hard on yourself

- Try to keep things in context.
- Remember that having a terrible day is a general human experience
- when your internal intellectual or an external scholar finds blames, try and

discover the truth and special case for what is being said

- If you stagger or feel you have fizzled, don't hit yourself.
- Go about as though you were your own closest friend: be caring and calm.
- Give yourself some time.

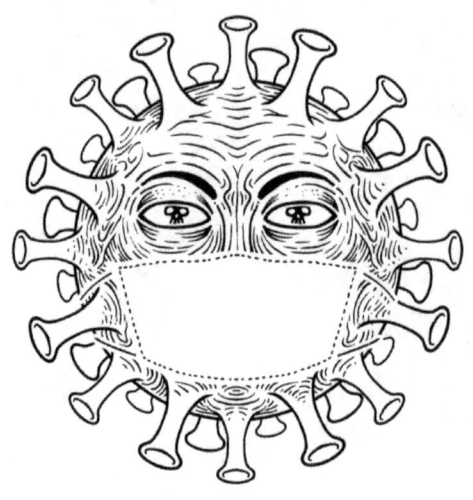

The pandemic virus, so named because they are crown-shaped, are a broad family of viruses that is frequent in several species of animals.

Mostly, these strains begin symptoms associated to the common cold but may sometimes graduate to higher complications of diseases of the lower respiratory tract, like pneumonia or bronchitis.

Rarely, animal pandemic viruses can develop and escalate amidst people, as it was noted in the cases of the MERS-CoV and SARS-CoV. The outbreak of this virus of late is still under investigation. Health experts presume that the advent of this virus has its source in large seafood and animal market from the Wuhan city that is widening to every human to human.

Pandemic viruses are a family of viruses that were discovered in the 1960s but whose origin is still unknown. Its different types cause different diseases, from a cold to a severe respiratory syndrome (a severe form of pneumonia).

Much of the pandemic viruses are not dangerous and can be treated effectively. In fact, most people get a pandemic virus at some time in their life, usually during their childhood. Although they are more frequent in autumn or winter, they can be purchased at any time of the year.

The pandemic virus owes its name to the appearance it presents since it is very similar to a crown or a halo. It is a type of virus present in both humans and animals.

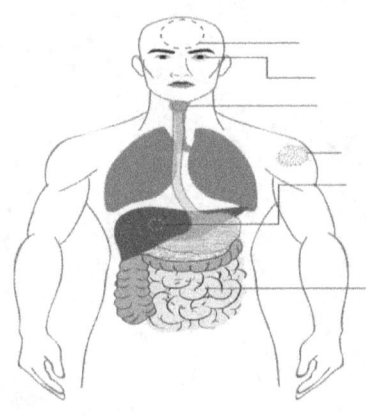

The pandemic virus spreads a little more each day. First confined to China (and, in particular, to the city of Wuhan, home of the epidemic), it spread throughout Asia before reaching the United States, Australia, and France - where 12 cases have so far been confirmed.

If for the moment, the health authorities are playing the appeasement card (the hospitals are ready, the organizational plans are well established, the screening test developed by the Pasteur Institute is effective), the Chinese president Xi Jinping speaks of an epidemic that "is accelerating "and a "serious" situation.

What are the symptoms to watch for?

In most countries, vigilance is required for travelers who have stayed in China recently - as a reminder; the pandemic virus epidemic began in late December 2019 and was officially declared in early January 2020. The main symptoms to watch out for if you have traveled to China, have fever and cough or shortness of breath.

- A fever above 37.5 ° C,
- A dry or oily cough,
- Respiratory signs such as cough, tightness, and / or chest pain, sometimes with shortness of breath (shortness of breath).
- Chills,

- Body aches,
- Unusual fatigue,
- Headaches.

And also: the symptoms described above also correspond to classic flu symptoms. If you haven't flown, if you haven't been to China recently, if you haven't stopped at an Asian airport, there's no need to panic!

How is the virus spread?

The majority of the cases initially described initially concern people who must have been to an animal market; scientists favor the hypothesis of a zoonosis (disease transmitted by animals). Also, person-to-person transmission has been proven: the new virus (responsible for the disease) spreads between humans by air, by direct contact with secretions or through a contaminated object - such as influenza. Clearly: we can catch the 2019-nCoV virus if we drink from the same glass as an infected person if we kiss him if he sneezes not far from us if he does not wash his hands and that we touch the same objects as him.

Transmission: the pangolin on the culprit bench. Have you ever heard of the pangolin? This small-scale mammal has, according to a study published by the University of Agriculture in southern China, facilitated the transmission of the 2019-nCoV virus from the bat to humans.

Explanation: if scientists are almost sure that the source of the epidemic is the bat (the "reservoir" in the jargon of specialists), the virus present in the latter could not have come directly to humans, lack of suitable receivers. It, therefore, lacked an "intermediate host": after having swept away the hypothesis of the snake, the experts looked into the pangolin. This resolutely exotic mammal (which is the subject of illegal trafficking in Asia with around 100,000 specimens poached each year) indeed presents viral sequences identical to 99% to those found in patients.

Please note: some scientists call for caution with this hypothesis - the evidence for which has not (yet) been published in the scientific literature.

To protect themselves from the virus, health authorities recommend barrier measures that have proven their worth against the influenza virus:

- Wash your hands frequently with soap,
- Cough and sneeze in the crook of his elbow, or in a disposable handkerchief,
- Avoid touching your face (nose, mouth ...etc.).

Is this virus dangerous? What are the risks?

To date, the most severe cases mainly concern people who are vulnerable because of their age or associated diseases. The available scientific data suggests that the virus can cause symptoms similar to those of moderate flu, but also more severe symptoms. In these cases, the patient may have acute respiratory distress syndrome, acute renal failure, or even multi-visceral failure, which can lead to death. You should know that 75% of people who died in China suffered from chronic pathologies, and 80% were elderly.

What is the incubation time?

The incubation period for the pandemic virus is 5 to 6 days on average, with variations ranging from 2 to 14 days. However, we do not know how long it can be detected in someone who is no longer sick. Nor even if a person can be contagious when he does not yet have symptoms.

Wearing a mask: a barrier gesture for patients

In large cities, particularly in Paris, the wearing of masks is becoming more and more common. So much so that some pharmacies are out of stock. The most commonly used masks, surgical masks, also called anti-splash masks, are recommended for people with symptomatic illnesses, that is to say, who cough or sneeze. The objective is to avoid the spread of the disease by postillions, therefore by air.

What is the pandemic virus?

These pandemic viruses are a family of viruses that can cause disease in animals and humans. In humans, they can cause respiratory infections ranging from a common cold to more serious illnesses, such as the Middle East respiratory syndrome (MERS) and severe acute respiratory syndrome (SARS).

We are currently facing a pandemic (an epidemic that is spread worldwide) by a new pandemic virus, SARS-CoV-2, which was recently discovered and caused the disease by the pandemic virus.

What are the symptoms of the virus?

People with the virus often have flu-like symptoms, such as fever, tiredness, and a dry cough.

Some people may have muscle aches, a stuffy nose, a sore throat, or diarrhea.

Most people (about 80%) recover from the disease in about seven days without the need for any special treatment. About 1 in 6 people who develop the virus can progress to serious illness and have difficulty breathing, which may require hospitalization.

Older people and those with underlying medical conditions, such as cardiovascular disease, respiratory disease, or weakened defenses, are at increased risk of developing a serious illness. People with fever, cough, and shortness of breath should seek medical attention immediately.

How long does the virus infection last?
The duration of the disease varies from person to person. Mild symptoms in a healthy individual can go away on their own within a few days, usually about a week. Similar to the flu, recovery for a person with other ongoing health problems, such as a respiratory condition, can take weeks and, in severe cases, complicate or be life-threatening.

What is the difference between the new virus and the flu?
The symptoms of the virus and the flu are generally very similar. Both cause fever and respiratory symptoms, which can range from mild to severe and sometimes fatal.

Both viruses are also transmitted in the same way, by coughing or sneezing, or by contact with the virus-contaminated hands, surfaces, or objects.

Washing your hands, covering yourself with a disposable tissue or with the crease of the elbow when coughing or sneezing, and a good cleaning of the home are important actions to prevent both infections.

The risk of serious illness appears to be higher for the virus than for the flu. While most people with the virus have mild symptoms, approximately 15% have severe infections, and 5% require intensive care.

How is the virus transmitted?

It is transmitted from one person to another through drops from the nose or mouth that are thrown when the infected person coughs, sneezes or speaks, by contact with contaminated hands, surfaces or objects.

That is why it is important to maintain social distance and take the contact precautions described below.

What can I do to avoid getting the virus?

To reduce the risk of contracting the virus, we suggest:

- Social distancing: avoid meetings, events and leaving the house in general, except for absolutely essential activities.
- Maintain hand hygiene by regularly cleaning them with soap and water or gel alcohol.

Clean your hands:

- before entering and leaving an area used by other people,
- after using the bathroom,
- after coughing or sneezing,
- before preparing food or eating.

- When coughing and sneezing, cover with disposable tissues (throw them away after use and wash your hands immediately afterward) or do it at the elbow crease if you don't have disposable tissues.
- Periodically clean surfaces and objects you use frequently.
- Ventilate the environments.

When should I wash my hands?

Handwashing is the easiest way to prevent many diseases, not just that of the new pandemic virus. It is important that you do so:

- Before I touch your face.
- After coughing or sneezing.
- After going to the bathroom.
- Before and after changing diapers.
- Before preparing and eating food.

- Before and after visiting or caring for someone who is sick.
- After throwing out the trash.
- After touching frequently used surfaces such as door handles, railings, handrails, etc.
- After being in public places or touching animals.

Why do I need to frequently wash my hands or use gel alcohol to prevent the spread of the new virus?

Washing your hands with soap and water or using an alcohol-based disinfectant removes any viral particles from your hands.

Why do I have to sneeze using the elbow crease and not the hand?

This prevents the spread of the virus. If it is done with our hands, we help the virus to spread to everything we touch.

Should I avoid shaking hands with the new pandemic virus?

Yes. Respiratory viruses can be spread by shaking hands and then touching your eyes, nose, and mouth. At this time, it is better to greet with a gesture or a tilt of the head rather than with the hand. I mean

Why do I have to keep a distance of at least 1 meter with another person?

When someone coughs or sneezes, they give off a few drops of liquid through their nose or mouth that may contain the virus. If that person has the disease and is too close to another, they can breathe the droplets and with them the new virus.

Why should I avoid touching my eyes, nose, and mouth?

The hands touch many surfaces and may contain the virus on their surface. Once contaminated, they can transfer the virus to the eyes, nose, or mouth. If the virus enters, it can cause the disease.

For this reason, it is important to wash your hands frequently or use gel alcohol.

What does it mean to be someone's contact with the new virus?

The following definition is dynamic and may vary over the course of the pandemic.

To date, any person who has been close (face to face for at least 15 minutes or in the same closed space for at least 2 hours) to a person who has a confirmed diagnosis of the new virus is considered a "contact."

What should I do if I come into close contact with a person with the new virus?

If you are identified as a contact of a person with a confirmed the new virus infection, you must reinforce your isolation for 14 days from the last contact with the confirmed case of the new virus, monitor your health, and report any symptoms. If you live with other people, in turn, you must strictly comply with the isolation within your home and not have close contact with any cohabitant, especially if the person is over 60 years old or is part of a risk group.

What should I do if I come into close contact with a person who was identified as the contact of another person with confirmed infection?

Close contact contacts do not carry a risk. If you were in contact with a person identified as a close contact of another person with infection confirmed by the new virus, you must maintain the same preventive social isolation that is followed by all of society, and continue with general measures to prevent the disease from the new pandemic virus. On the other hand, it is recommended that you pay special attention to warning signs or the appearance of symptoms, however slight they may be.

What does social distancing mean?
Social distancing means:

- that you leave a distance of at least 1 meter between you and others;
- that you avoid crowds and mass gatherings where it is difficult to maintain adequate distance from others;
- to avoid small gatherings in closed spaces, such as family celebrations;
- that you avoid shaking hands, hugging or kissing other people;
- that you do not share the mate, tableware, and utensils;

- to avoid visiting vulnerable people, such as those in nursing homes or hospitals, babies, or people with compromised immune systems due to illness or medical treatment.

You can commute to work on public transportation if you have no other way. Please try to maintain social distance with other passengers.

Social distancing is an effective measure, but it is recognized that it cannot be practiced in all situations; its objective is to reduce the transmission potential. Keep in mind that, in this sense, in some jurisdictions, the use of masks, masks, or homemade chinstraps is compulsory in means of transport or shops to support social distancing measures.

It is important that we all do our part to limit the spread of the new virus while complying with social, preventive and mandatory isolation; This will help protect vulnerable people in our community and reduce the burden on hospitals.

Why is social distancing important?

Social distancing is the best measure we can take to decrease the circulation of the SARS-CoV2 pandemic virus, causing the new virus disease.

You must bear in mind that it is not always possible to achieve absolute social distancing. In any case, we strongly recommend you try to do it in order to protect yourself and others.

Is it useful to use a homemade chinstrap?

Staying at home, keeping social distance, and washing our hands several times a day are the best-known measures so far to prevent the pandemic virus. However, the use of homemade chinstraps can also help decrease the risk of transmission when these measures cannot be assured. For more information, see the section on Using Home Chinstrap.

Is there a cure or a vaccine?

So far, there are no vaccines that protect against the new virus. There is also no specific treatment.

Early diagnosis and general supportive care are important. Most of the time, the symptoms resolve on their own. People who have serious illnesses with complications may need to be seen in the hospital.

Is the flu vaccine useful against the pandemic virus?

No, the flu shot only prevents influenza. There is still no vaccine against the pandemic virus, which is why prevention is so important.

In any case, it is very important that the flu risk groups (older adults, people with respiratory problems, health personnel) get the flu vaccine every year.

Can the new virus be treated?
Infections caused by new pandemic viruses do not have a specific treatment, although the symptoms it causes can be treated. The treatment of the symptoms will depend on the clinical state of each patient.

Are there people who present more risks if they are infected?
Yes. People over the age of 60, those with respiratory or cardiovascular diseases, and those with conditions such as diabetes are at higher risk for infection.

When is a case considered suspicious?

The definition is dynamic and varies over time.

Is a blood test or other biological sample done to find out if a person has contracted the new pandemic virus?

No. The diagnosis must be made in the reference laboratories in clinical respiratory samples. The recommendations of the Ministry of Health of the Nation are those that establish which people should carry out the corresponding studies.

How long is the new virus incubation period?

The "incubation period" is the time between infection by the virus and the appearance of symptoms of the disease, which according to the available data, ranges from 1 to 14 days, and on average, around five days. For comparison, the incubation period for influenza is 2 days on average and ranges from 1 to 7. For this reason, people who may have been in contact with a confirmed case are asked to isolate themselves for 14 days.

Can my companion animal infect me with the new virus?

Although there was a case of an infected dog in Hong Kong, to date, there is no evidence that a dog, cat, or any pet can transmit the new virus or that these animals can become sick from a human. Likewise, research and knowledge about this new disease continue.

In addition, it is important to take some care when removing pets so that they can relieve themselves during preventive and compulsory social isolation.

Where can I find updated and truthful information about the new virus?

In the era of communications, disinformation is common and dangerous. Events such as the pandemic by the new virus put us in need of obtaining information instantly; for this reason, the spread of false or erroneous content is frequent.

It is our responsibility to prevent the spread of false or malicious information. It is key that we do not act as amplifiers of fake news, which generally seek rapid emotional impact for their virtualization.

To avoid confusion, you should search for information on social network accounts that allow verifying their veracity, such as those of the Ministry of Health of the Argentine Republic, the World Health Organization, or the Pan American Health Organization.

Be suspicious of - and don't spread - WhatsApp rumors, messages, and audios from alleged authorities on the matter that spread information that cannot be verified.

Recommendations for home cleaning and personal care

How long does the virus survive on a surface?

Studies (including available preliminary information on the new virus indicate that pandemic viruses can subsist on a surface for a few hours to several days.

The time may vary depending on the conditions (for example, the type of surface, the temperature or the humidity of the environment).

Cleaning with a common disinfectant, washing your hands, using alcohol gel, and avoiding touching your eyes, mouth, or nose reduces the risk of transmission.

What cleaning products to choose, and what care must be taken?

For cleaning, it is recommended to use traditional, simple, and cheap products such as detergent. Water and detergent are suitable as long as you scrub well and remove any visible material or dirt.

Before using a cleaning product, read the label carefully, and follow the rules of use and protection indicated on the packaging, checking the expiration date.

And remember that pregnant women or people with respiratory conditions such as asthma or others are especially delicate against cleaning chemicals.

What should I keep in mind when choosing and using a cleaning product?

Whatever the product, you should always check its expiration date before using it. Use it following the manufacturer's instructions as its misuse can be dangerous, or decrease or nullify its effectiveness. Products should not be diluted or mixed together unless indicated on the packaging.

What percentage of bleach and water should I use to disinfect my home?

After cleaning floors and surfaces with water and detergent, or the product you use regularly, it is recommended to disinfect with bleach. You should add 10 ml of bleach (2 tablespoons) for every liter of water or 100 ml of bleach for every 10 liters of water (one cup of coffee in a bucket of water approximately). It must be bleach for domestic use (with a concentration of 55 gram/liter). If using a commercial bleach with a concentration of 25 g / l, the double volume of bleach must be placed to achieve proper disinfection. It should be prepared the same day that it is going to be used if it does not lose the power of the disinfectant.

How should I clean surfaces and floors to avoid the new virus?

Cleaning surfaces and floors can be done correctly by following these three steps:

1. Wash with a solution of water and detergent.

2. Rinse with clean water.

3. Disinfect with a solution of 10 ml (2 tablespoons) of bleach (with a concentration of 55 gram/liter) in 1 liter of water. If using commercial bleach with a concentration of 25 g / l, double the volume of bleach should be placed to achieve proper disinfection.

Can I mix different cleaning products like detergent and bleach?

You should never mix detergent with bleach. This combination can release poisonous vapors that affect health. If cleaning with detergent, it must be rinsed with clean water before disinfecting with bleach.

What personal care should I have when cleaning the home?

Try to use the usual rubber gloves to avoid hand contact with cleaning products. As general care, you should avoid splashing on the face, and once cleaning is finished, wash your hands with soap and water.

Does bleach serve to disinfect my hands if I don't have soap?

Yes, a low concentration bleach or bleach solution (0.05%) can be used. It should be used only if you do not have soap or alcohol-based hand sanitizer. It should not be used often because it can irritate the hands and affect health.

Is it the same to use soap as detergent to wash my hands?

Although detergent can clean hands, its components make it very strong for the skin, so it is convenient to use ordinary hand soap.

Do all soaps work?

Yes, all soaps work, even soap on white bread. The virus has three layers, one of which and the main one is fat. Soaps remove this fat and destroy the other layers that compose it.

If I have a bucket of bleach water, can all family members wash our hands there?

No. It is important that we always wash with clean soapy water. If we do not have running water, we can use a plastic bottle, fill it with drinking or purified water and loosen the cap a little so that a small splash of water comes out when the bottle is upside down. Another person has to hold the bottle while you wash your hands with soap under the water. (Used water can be collected in a bucket and used for the bathroom, for example.)

How can I make the water drinkable?

In addition to the drinking water supplied by the network (running water), you can turn into safe water that comes from other sources (well, cistern, cistern, etc.).

In that case, add 2 drops of bleach (with a concentration of 55 gram/liter), per liter of water (and let it rest for at least 30 minutes before consuming it) or boil for three minutes, either drinking water, washing the hands or teeth, cooking or washing vegetables and fruits. If using a commercial bleach with a concentration of 25 g / l, double the volume of bleach should be placed to achieve proper disinfection.

How should I clean fruits and vegetables?

If raw fruits and vegetables are to be consumed, wash them with water to remove dirt and impurities. Then, you can disinfect them by immersing them in water with 1.5ml (approximately half a teaspoon) of bleach per liter of water (leaving to act for 20 minutes). It must be bleach for domestic use (with a concentration of 55 gram/liter). Rinse again thoroughly with plenty of water before consuming.

How to disinfect objects of daily use (such as cell phones, keys, doorknobs, etc.)?

To clean the cell phone, you can use cloth or cloth and alcohol. Cell phone cases and other plastic objects can be washed with soap and water or detergent. The handles, handles, keys, and metal elements can be cleaned with a cloth with diluted bleach (2 tablespoons in 1 liter of water if it is bleach with a concentration of 55gr / liter, to use commercial bleach with a concentration of 25 g / l, the double volume of bleach should be placed). It is recommended to clean them daily.

How do I have to wash the sheets and towels?

Wash bed linens and towels with soaps or standard detergents, and then ideally dry them in sunlight before using them again.

Inside my house, should we maintain social distance?

In your house, try to avoid direct contact with other people as much as possible: hugging, shaking hands, kissing, etc. If there are boys and girls, other ways of expressing affection and closeness can be created with them through games, etc.

Also remember not to share the mate, the cutlery, the plates, and glasses, among others.

What should I do if I receive purchases that I made by phone or the internet?

In the case of receiving packages that have been handled, transported, and exposed to different conditions and by different people, we suggest you carry out the recommended disinfection procedure.

Travel information

I traveled to a country considered high risk for the new virus, what do I have to do?

If you were, left, or traveled through a country with the new virus circulation in the last 14 days, you must isolate yourself from others for 14 days from the day you left the affected country, and monitor yourself for symptoms. There are jurisdictions that have specific protocols for people arriving on travel on authorized flights.

If you develop fever or respiratory symptoms, even if they are mild, contact the health system.

In case of respiratory distress, or if your symptoms are severe, call 911 immediately identifying yourself, inform the staff where you traveled or if you were in contact with a confirmed case.

If you have symptoms, it is important that you do not go to work, maintain the isolation and social distance of your cohabitants until you are evaluated, even if you are part of the essential staff.

I traveled to a country that is not considered at risk for the new virus, what do I have to do?

If you traveled to another country in the last 14 days, regardless of which country, you should self-monitor for symptoms, practice social distancing and social isolation, preventive and mandatory.

If you develop fever or respiratory symptoms, even if they are mild, please contact the health system.

In case of respiratory distress, or if the symptoms are severe, call 911, inform the staff where you traveled or if you were in contact with a confirmed case.

If you have symptoms, it is important that you do not go to work even if you are part of the essential staff.

Can I take a trip?

Currently, according to the regulations of preventive and compulsory social isolation, no trips can be made.

CHAPTER 6 –EFFECTS THE PANDEMIC VIRUS CAUSES: STRESS, ANXIETY, AND DEPRESSION

Collective stress in pandemic virus period

In this period, when we are struck by the pandemic called a pandemic virus, it is important to point out that there is a percentage of vulnerability to suffering from stress, anxiety, so, as a cardiologist, I allow myself to make some recommendations to our patient population.

There are symptoms such as inability to concentrate, upset stomach, sleep problems, headaches, mood changes, which may be translating into stress due to the current situation. But, just like this time, it is important to notify your doctor of symptoms or signs that persist, which can lead to elevated blood pressure, increased inflammation of the body, higher levels of cholesterol and triglycerides, palpitations (arrhythmias), among others.

We tend under stress to do things harmful to our body, such as increasing the intake of sugar, fats, salt, sedentary lifestyle, hyper-information in networks, or the media, which can have an impact on our cardiovascular health.

If you have psychological or psychiatric-type pathologies, the right thing to do is to talk to your doctor, avoid worsening them, not make decisions to increase or stop drugs.

Try as a cardiovascular or cardio metabolic patient to follow your doctor's recommendations, lead a healthy life at home, spend your time reading books, meditating, praying, organizing, developing new projects, making virtual communication with families or friends, disconnecting from networks or the media at certain times during the day.

Stress can lead to creating symptoms without having the condition (pandemic virus) or (cardiovascular pathologies), but if you have them, the right communication with your doctor is the right thing to do.

Find out if you need virtual therapy help if needed.

Those who are able to assume or rule out diagnoses are health professionals; please allow communication between them and you.

Remember, first of all, stay at home!

Signs to recognize when stress becomes dangerous to health

There is a type of stress that is positive, and it is the one that allows us to adapt to daily challenges and demands. But there is a point where it can become harmful. How to know when to act to remedy it

Stress is a set of reactions of the body to challenges or demands. It is a natural process that responds to our need to adapt to the environment. Contrary to what many believe, there is a type of stress that is positive and occurs in small episodes, such as when it helps to be alert and avoid a certain danger or meet a deadline. However, it becomes detrimental to health when it is very intense or increases over time.

According to a study published by The American Journal of Cardiology, people with a high level of stress have a 27% higher risk of suffering from heart disease. This indicates that stress is clearly one more risk factor to control, as do high blood pressure and high cholesterol. Therefore, it is extremely important to pay attention to it since it can affect our health if it is installed in our daily life.

Men and women are vulnerable to stress, although both experience it in different ways. Medical studies confirmed that stress does not affect everyone in the same way and that while women are more likely than men to show symptoms of heart difficulty after stressful situations and emotional shocks.

Breaking up with a partner, losing a family member, or a strong argument can trigger what is known as "broken heart syndrome," where the main affected are usually post-menopausal women between 55 and 75 years old.

Dr. Alejandro Deviggiano is the coordinator of the Department of Non-Invasive

Cardiovascular Studies of Maipú Diagnosis and detailed the most common symptoms that stress usually causes, which can be physical and emotional.

"In some cases, you may not realize that these symptoms are caused by stress, " he said, listing some of the most frequent signs: emotions (depression or anxiety, irritability, fear), thoughts (excessive fear failure, excessive self-criticism, forgetfulness, difficulty concentrating), behaviors (a rough treatment of others, increased consumption of tobacco, alcohol and other drugs), physical changes (muscle tension, cold or sweaty hands, insomnia, headaches, indigestion).

Likewise, the specialists emphasize the fact that "it is important to bear in mind that constant stress can strain the heart in various ways, increasing cholesterol and triglyceride levels in the blood and increasing blood pressure." Also, extreme stress can make your heartbeat out of rhythm.

In this sense, knowing the different types of stress is necessary to know when to act to remedy it:

-Acute stress: it is the most common form of stress. It arises from the demands that we impose ourselves or others. It occurs in short periods, usually due to a passing cause, such as a trip, exam, or job change. In small doses, it can be positive, but in higher doses, it can affect our health, causing muscle aches, stomach, and intestinal problems, temporary overexcitation, headaches, and exhaustion.

-Chronic stress: it is the most exhausting and exhausting type of stress. It takes place when one does not find a way out of a problem or situation that depresses him. It is the product, for example, of an unwanted job or career, money problems, or an unhappy marriage. Unlike acute stress, it occurs over and over repeatedly over time. It produces physical and psychological wear and tear, which can trigger depression, nervous breakdown, and even a heart attack.

Knowing the different types of stress is necessary to know when to act to remedy it

"Coping with stress will allow us to lead a better quality of life," said Deviggiano, noting that "in addition to eating healthy, sleeping well and exercising, it is advisable to consider the following techniques":

-Recognize and accept things that cannot be changed; let them go. For example, you can't change the fact of having to drive during rush hour, but you can find ways to relax on the road, such as listening to favorite music or an audio book.

-Change perspective. Try to develop a more positive attitude towards challenges. You can always see the "glass half full."

-Learn ways to relax. It helps to decrease heart rate and lower blood pressure. There are many ways, from deep breaths and meditation to yoga.

-Connect with loved ones. Don't let stress get in the way of social life. Spending time with family and friends can help you feel better. Trusting problems with a friend can also help solve them.

-Learn to say no. If stress is caused by doing too many tasks at home or at work, setting limits is critical to balance.

The new virus: tips for managing stress during confinement

Stress is the body's reaction to physical or environmental pressure. Whether we are confined alone or with family, whether we are telecommuting or forced to go to our place of work... the period is favorable to feeling stressed.

Staying active

Exercise helps fight stress because it releases the hormone endorphins. To stay active during the confinement period, the AFC invites you to carry out an achievable health routine several times a day, whatever your physical condition.

For the more athletic, deprived of their training ... search the Internet, which is full of videos of various activities (Hiit, Zumba, Pilates ...) accessible at any level and for free. Be careful, however, to practice with caution and not to overload your muscles and joints.

For you, as for the health professionals mobilized by the pandemic virus, it would be a question of not injuring yourself.

Keep in touch

Stress and isolation do not mix well. New technologies are precious in this period. Exchanges in audio or video, two or more, our smart phones offer us endless possibilities to keep in touch with our loved ones.

If you have no one to turn to, why not look into support groups or hotlines. On the Internet and social networks, you can easily find self-help groups!

Take time for yourself

If some people currently suffer from loneliness and isolation, others, on the contrary, find it increasingly difficult to be locked up with their spouse and children.

 Under these conditions, to take a step back and have fun, allow yourself time to listen to music, take a bath, watch a movie, or read

... Identify what brings you the most pleasure, the most relaxation, and sanction this moment.

Avoid the exciting

Alcohol, tobacco, caffeine, if they soothe you at the time produce in the medium term the opposite of the expected effect. However, if you have an addiction to alcohol, tobacco, or any other substance, do not set a withdrawal goal without being accompanied.

Helping others

Develop his resilience, feeling gratitude, helping his neighbor helps him fight his own stress, and there is currently a lot to do to help the most vulnerable in the situation of confinement.

It is for this reason that the Government mobilizes the civic reserve to carry out four essential missions: food and emergency aid to the most deprived; childcare for caregivers or foster children; the link with isolated people (calling missions of the elderly or sick); local solidarity (for shopping for fragile neighbors).

Breathing Exercise to Combat Stress

This breathing exercise can help you deal with stress, anxiety, or panic. It only takes a few minutes and can be done anywhere. You can indeed do it sitting, standing, or lying down.

 Lying down, place your arms slightly away from your body, palms up. Extend your legs or bend your knees with your feet on the floor, whichever is more comfortable for you. Sitting, place your arms on the armrests. Sit or stand, place your feet flat on the floor, away from your hip width. Once comfortably installed, you can start the breathing exercise:

Breathe in deeply, swelling the stomach, without forcing. It must remain comfortable. Inhale through the nose and exhale through the mouth, quietly and regularly. To maintain a regular rhythm, some people find it easier to mentally count four beats, both inhalation, and inhalation.

Breathe, counting, or not, for 3 to 5 minutes.

How long does it take to form a habit?

A habit is a learned behavior that remains as a routine or as an acquired skill. But how long does the action take to become a habit? Let's see in this section what recent research in this field says and how to speed up this process.

What is a habit?

Habits are automatic behaviors; gestures you perform without even realizing it.

With such a definition, they could look like something completely negative. After all,

148

growth passes through the eradication of automatisms and is oriented towards a more conscious life, in which you are increasingly present in what you do, without automatisms.

In this scenario, habits would seem to be totally banned.

But is it really so?

Is it possible to live without habits?

Above all, would it be useful?

The advantages of habits

Our attention span and **our ability to consciously process the actions we perform are limited**. That is, we have limited mental resources, which we can use to carry out the task we are doing.

It is true that these **abilities** can be increased considerably, but still remains finite; they **are not infinite**.

Bringing a gesture to an unconscious level allows you to **free your attention from the**

task of elaborating that gesture and consciously channeling it towards an action you choose.

In ordinary life, almost half of the actions we perform are carried out in this way.

A study [1] of about ten years ago estimated that **about 45% of our behavior is dictated by habits**, by routines that we carry out automatically.

If these actions were done consciously, there would be very little cognitive space to do anything else.

When the habit becomes automated, it moves into **a mental space called "cognitive unconscious."** Let's see some examples to better understand this passage.

Brush your teeth

The habit of brushing teeth is a behavior that, once learned, you perform without having to think about it, without having to remember to do it.

It is not an action rooted in the nature of the human being. It was learned or taught to us as children.For me, brushing teeth is a healthy habit, but for my 5-year-old daughter, it is still not. It is still in the learning phase of a habit.For me, it is not exhausting, and I don't forget it. It is an automatic gesture that I make after eating at meals. It doesn't require any effort.

It's different for my daughter; she doesn't have this habit. If I don't remember it if you forget it. And while she does it, she does it thinking about brushing her front teeth, her back teeth, etc. This requires a certain amount of effort.

Type on the keyboard

Right now, I'm typing on the keyboard, and my hands run over the keys without me having to pay attention to them. In this way, my mind is free to think, and the action of translating my thought into text happens automatically.

This is possible because I learned the habit of typing on the keyboard without looking at the keys. The process of translating thought into digital text occurs by itself, on an unconscious level. **My awareness can thus turn entirely in elaborating the message I want to communicate to you.**

If I had to pay attention to each key, I press, my ability to process the thought I want to communicate to you would be greatly reduced. Part of my attention would be engaged in typing the keys one by one, looking for them on the keyboard, and being careful not to make mistakes.

Driving

When you drive your car, while being busy driving, you have the ability to talk to someone.

If you were to bring all your conscious attention to the gestures necessary to keep the car on the road without making accidents, you would really struggle to converse with a person by your side.

And in fact, that's exactly what happens when you learn to drive. You cannot be distracted in the least because you are learning a new habit, the commitment is maximum, and all your awareness is focused on learning.

And have you ever wondered why, when you park, the gesture of lowering the volume of the radio comes naturally to you?

Because in the parking maneuver, you need more concentration. You need this to regain awareness of an action you take automatically because you know that more attention is required.

Then instinctively turn down - or turn off - the radio. In this way, you **recover the workspace in your awareness** to elaborate on the precise gestures required in the parking lot.

Summing up

The advantage of performing an action in the form of habit, this as an automatic gesture, is that:

- Allows you to have free attention to use consciously.
- Allows you to quickly and fluidly perform actions that, if done consciously, would be slow.

Choose your habits consciously.

We have seen how **habits can be both positive and negative**.

In themselves, they have nothing wrong; they are not an element to be banned from our life. Indeed, they are an element on which to bring attention to grow as a person. How?

By consciously choosing your habits.

What are those actions that, repeated in your daily life, can create a long-term benefit?
 These should become habits to be cultivated intentionally.

Just think about physical activity: we know very well how beneficial it is, and we also know that to have real positive consequences, it must be practiced constantly. If you have a habit of exercising regularly, this becomes automatic over time that brings health in the long run.

When it becomes a habit, you don't have to motivate yourself every day to do the physical activity; you do it spontaneously, it's part of your daily life, it doesn't require your effort or motivation.

So, a message to take home from reading this section is:

Consciously choose which virtuous behaviors you would like in your life, and make them a habit.

Bad habits

In that 45% of actions that we perform in the form of habits, there are both behaviors that are useful to you, and others that are dysfunctional.

They are "bad habits."

They are the **daily routines** that, in the long run, determine an **impoverishment of your quality of life**.

It is often difficult to abandon bad habits because they **are deeply rooted** in us. They are the result of years of repetition and therefore have left an important furrow from which it is often difficult to get out.

An important principle in dealing with dysfunctional habits is this:

Bad habits are not eliminated; they are replaced.

The invitation is not to fight negative automatic behaviors, but **to ensure that new habits replace those that you do not consider suitable**.

The choice and the will to learn a new habit are a starting point, but they do not have the guarantee of the result in themselves. By themselves, they are not enough; you need a system that allows you to acquire this behavior in your life.

The learning of a habit inevitably passes **through the repetition of the behavior** one wants to learn, **for a time sufficient to make it become a routine.**

But how long does it take to form a habit?

The myth of the 21 days

From the 1960s, the idea began to spread that it **was enough to repeat an action every day for 21 consecutive days** to definitively learn a habit.

The idea originated from what **Maxwell Maltz** wrote in his book **Psycho-Cybernetics**.

 Maltz was a plastic surgeon, and he observed, observing his patients, that it usually took **three weeks to adapt to a physical change**, such as amputation of an arm.

Since then, 21 has become a magical number, hailed as a goal that, once reached, allows you to keep a habit.

The idea that has long been widespread is that, for example, just going for a run 21 days in a row to then have this habit for life without any effort.

It is a principle that has, as its foundation, the observation of a single case: the patients of dr. Maltz.

It may be true for them, **but the reality of things is more complex**, because:

- **each of us is different**
- **every habit is different**
- life inserts **unpredictable variables**

We can then take this magic number and put it in the "urban legends" category.

Why does it sometimes work?

The **simple habits** require little effort and repetition to be learned.

Having a deadline, such as the three weeks of Maltz, to which the **belief of success is** firmly associated, often has a positive response. Facilitates learning.

Having reached this **goal,** the person is convinced that he has triggered a permanent change, and this acts as a **positive**

reinforcement compared to the initial decision to maintain a routine.

Reaching a goal feeds the person's sense of **self - efficacy**, and **self - esteem**.

Precisely for these reasons, the magic number 21 still survives to the present day.

To observe the question from a more concrete point of view, let's see what contemporary research tells us in this field.

Real studies on learning habits

A scientific study studied a sample of people to determine how long it took to learn a habit.

The conclusion is that there is no magic number: there is **great subjective variability.**

For some people, **18 days** were enough to pass an automatic action, for others **more than eight months.**

The study group average was **66 days.**

66 isn't a new magic number; it's just the average of this study group.

To draw a practical conclusion from this research, we can say that **months of effort are usually required** to learn a habit.

The wide individual variability derives from the complexity of the habit to be learned and from our personal characteristics.

But what is the element that makes an action a habit?

When can we say that it has become a learned behavior?

From habit to skill

The process of learning a consciously chosen habit **is equivalent to that of learning a skill.**

We pass from an **initial condition** in which a **great effort** is required to carry out an activity. As the repetitions of correct behavior increase, **the effort to perform the gesture also decreases**.

Behavior becomes **a** learned **skill** when it **is performed spontaneously, with minimal cognitive effort**.

It has become your ability, **your way of being in life**. This **is equivalent to having intentionally learned a habit**.

Let's see an example.

Don't interrupt

Suppose you have a habit of interrupting the other while he is speaking, and that you want to change it because you understand that this gesture affects understanding. Choose to acquire the ability not to interrupt (the new good habit you want to acquire).

The process is not instantaneous: the first few times, you will find it hard not to interrupt because the ingrained habit will make itself heard in a loud voice.

The more you repeat the correct action you want to learn (do not interrupt)**, the more the effort required decreases.**

This goes on **to the point where you acquire the ability** not to interrupt the other while speaking. **You simply do it**. It's your way of interacting with each other, and you don't have to pay attention to us. Do not interrupt has become your habit in dialogue with each other. Being a habit, you do it without even realizing it.

This frees your attention, which can now be conveyed, for example, in trying to better understand the meaning of what the other is saying to you.

As long as part of your attention is engaged in trying not to interrupt, you don't have all your attention at your disposal in fully understanding communication.

When the skill is learned, awareness is free to devote himself entirely to dialogue.

Time doesn't count; repetitions count.

Time passes is not the magic ingredient that forms a habit, or that allows you to learn a skill.

It doesn't matter if 21 days, 30 or 90 passes. What makes the difference is **the frequency and intention** with which you repeat your behavior.

In 21 days, you can perform the same action 10, 21, 100 times.

It is the frequency that makes the difference.

The ability is not internalized with the passage of time but is learned at the time of execution.

The more executions you do, the more this ability is assimilated and eventually becomes a habit that you possess with skill.

The first repetitions require effort, and the **more this skill is internalized, the more the effort in the execution is lowered.**

Instead of asking yourself, "how long does it take to form a habit?" Try asking yourself, "How many reps do I need to learn a skill?"

Your current habits, healthy or bad, have been internalized after hundreds, if not thousands, of often daily repetitions.

The new skills you want to have in your life require the same frequency. **You have to sequence a series of intentional behaviors, with constancy and regularity, until the voluntary commitment falls below the skill line.**

How long does it take? It depends on the frequency and conscious commitment with which you repeat that action.

It does not depend on the time that passes, and it is up to you.

As you can see, the more the frequency of the action increases, the more the learning curve is lowered and shortened, from the time standpoint, than from the point of view of the commitment required.

The message to take home from this chapter about habits is this: **choose the new skills you want to possess and practice them regularly and constantly as long as you feel you have them completely as your usual way of being in life.**

Diet in times of the pandemic virus

Currently, there is no specific nutritional treatment for the new virus. These experts assure that the feeding guidelines are aimed at alleviating the symptoms generated by fever and respiratory problems, ensuring adequate hydration.

Thus, this document presents **seven food and nutrition recommendations** to be followed by the entire Spanish population. It focuses, in particular, on patients with the new virus with mild symptoms at home. In addition, it makes some recommendations on food and nutrition in critically ill patients admitted to the ICU.

Recommendations

1. **Maintain good hydration**. The recommendation of fluid intake is essential, and water consumption should be guaranteed on-demand (depending on the sensation of thirst) or even without such sensation, especially in older people, guaranteeing at least 1.8 liters of liquid per day, always preferring water as a source of hydration.

2. **Take at least 5 servings of fruit and vegetables a day.** Guaranteeing a consumption of at least 3 servings of fruit per day and 2 of vegetables is an objective to be met for the entire population, and of course,

also for people with the new virus with mild symptoms at home.

3. **Choose the consumption of whole-grain products and legumes.** It is recommended to choose whole grains from whole grain (whole wheat bread, whole-wheat pasta, brown rice), and stewed or stewed legumes, trying to cook these foods with vegetables.

4. **Choose dairy products (fermented milks/yogurt), preferably low in fat.** Currently, there is controversy about whether or not to recommend skimmed dairy products; the Academy seems more cautious to continue recommending skimmed dairy for adults. When talking about the recommendation of consuming fermented milks such as yogurt, kefir, etc., reference is made only to the natural type, not the rest of

the flavored, flavored, fruit varieties, etc., since they contain a significant amount of added sugar. There is no evidence that the consumption of fermented dairy helps in any way in defenses and to prevent or decrease the risk of infection.

5. **Moderate consumption of other foods of animal origin.** Consumption of meats (3-4 times a week, but maximum 1 time a week red meat - beef, lamb or pork), fish (2-3 times a week), eggs (3-4 times a week), and cheeses must be made within the framework of a healthy diet, preferably choosing poultry meats (chicken, turkey, etc.), rabbit and the lean of other animals such as pork, and avoiding the consumption of sausages, cold cuts and meats fats from any animal.

6. **Choose the consumption of nuts, seeds, and olive oil.** Olive oil is the dressing fat and cooked par excellence in the Spanish

Mediterranean diet. Nuts (almonds, walnuts, etc.) and seeds (sunflower, pumpkin, etc.) are also an excellent option as long as they are natural or toasted, avoiding fried, sweetened, and salted nuts.

7. **Avoid pre-cooked foods and fast food.** The consumption of pre-cooked foods (croquettes, pizzas, lasagna, cannelloni, etc.) and fast food (pizzas, hamburgers, etc.) are not generally recommended for healthy eating, and in particular for the youngest at home. Due to its high energy density (due to its high content of fats and/or sugars), its consumption is not recommended in general, and therefore neither in periods of isolation or home quarantine because they can increase the risk of being overweight or obesity and other associated pathologies. Decreased physical exercise and sedentary behaviors during confinement and an

unhealthy diet could increase the risk of chronic diseases.

Myths and truths about food and the pandemic virus: what to eat in these days of quarantine

First off, I am going to clarify that there is no miracle food, drink, or product that somehow prevents or cures the pandemic virus. The only way to prevent it is with social isolation. The variety and balance of food are important; this does not mean that you have to spend a fortune buying large quantities of the most expensive food. Small portions variety is the key.

What can we add from food? We can be better immunized, strengthen the defenses, to be able to face this type of infection, any virus or bacteria in general.

How do we do it? Incorporating some key nutrients, such as vitamin A, vitamin C, vitamin E, vitamin D, and some minerals such as magnesium, calcium, and zinc.

Drinking water and being hydrated is essential to eliminate toxins

It seems difficult, but it is a diet in which the same foods as always will be included, fruits of different colors and especially in season, dried fruits, seeds, legumes, and fundamentally water, which is very important for the lymphatic system to eliminate toxins. Incorporating fish can be in the form of tuna or hake filet that will help because omega 3 will reinforce defenses and common sense.

Rest is key. Stress affects the immune system; therefore, it is necessary not to panic but to be informed.

What is there to eat?

- Vegetables, vegetables, and seasonal fruits of different colors. Whenever possible, raw
- Dairy and eggs
- Whole grains and legumes

To meals add seeds

- Dried fruits, seeds and oils

- Lean meats, fish, especially trying to eat twice a week

- Important: mega doses of vitamin C does not have scientific evidence that it prevents diseases caused by any virus

Take advantage that you are at home and eat homemade. It complements a good and varied, balanced diet, including all food groups and also good hygiene, both in the kitchen and in the hands.

6 non-perishable foods that will last you all the quarantine

If you plan to fill your cupboard with a single trip to the supermarket for quarantine, we recommend that you mainly buy these foods. One of the most important recommendations for not getting the pandemic virus and not spreading it everywhere is to stay at home and limit all the activities of going to the supermarket, the store, or buying the pantry, so the quarantine can be somewhat complicated.

So many people are choosing to order app-made food, fast food, or processed foods that can ultimately hurt you a lot; however, there aren't many options for nourishing yourself properly with the limitations of not going out. But do not worry, because there are several non-perishable foods that can last for many years without rotting, spoiling or losing nutritional properties, in addition to the fact that some of them do not take up much space in your pantry.

Best of all, these can be included in healthy diets, prepare multiple dishes, and complement your diet without any risk without risking your health.

Therefore, here we list 10 essential foods that you must have in your pantry and that will last you all the quarantine:

1 - Legumes

Chickpeas or lentils can be kept in perfect condition for a long time, about a year or two. Thanks to the fact that its low amount of water prevents microbes from performing their vital functions, preserving their integrity.

2 - Rice - essential for quarantine

It is one of the most basic and popular foods that can be found in any supermarket or corner store, also, because it is dry and contain hardly any water, it can be kept for a long time in your pantry.

3 - Olives

The heat treatments used for processing and the cover liquid prevent the growth of microbes, so unopened pot olives last up to three years in the pantry.

4 - Tuna and other preserves for quarantine

Because canned foods are sealed, they can last up to four years in good condition. Mainly the tuna is cooked first so that all the enzymes die. The process of canned tuna removes all oxygen, allowing the container to be hermetically sealed.

5 - Potatoes

An essential food in the Mexican diet that, in addition to being very versatile and able to be prepared in many ways, is an ideal supplement for quarantine. Because it contains a high amount of sugar and very little water, bacteria do not harm potatoes, and they can be preserved without problems.

6 - Flour - versatile for quarantine

The flour is very cheap and is used to prepare all kinds of dough and dishes, as well as to coat meat and fish. Properly stored, most types of flour are valid for 6 or 8 months. Variants such as whole wheat flour and special flours, such as proprietary yeast flour, which has additional mixed ingredients, have a shorter shelf life of 4 to 6 months.

How to learn while in quarantine

In a matter of days, the pandemic virus did what the most progressive companies planned to spend years and millions of investments on - transferred many employees to remote work and forced them to quickly introduce flexible management models.

So far, this has caused a lot of inconveniences: dozens of new workgroups and chaos in messengers, endless online meetings, and difficult negotiations with the family about a convenient workspace in the apartment. But the costs of shock switching to the remote format will soon pass. Most companies will switch to a more productive rhythm of work in conditions of social distance. Employees will have more free time.

How to use the freed-up time for the benefit of yourself and the company? And what is the difference between a familiar education and quarantined education?

· During the quarantine period, employee responsibility for their own development increases. Waiting for the employer to tell you how to use the new tools for remote work (Teams, Trello, Jira, and many others) is too big a luxury today. To master these skills, you do not need to take courses and training

- the principle of training in production works better. All instructions can be found on the Internet or from more experienced colleagues.

· Any crisis requires not only necessary, but also excessive knowledge, because today one may be needed, and tomorrow another. Therefore, education should be redundant, go beyond narrow specialization. For example, it is important for managers to improve their digital communication and crisis communication skills, train their psychological resilience, and develop critical thinking. Some time ago, we introduced a humanitarian block into programs and developed these abilities in the process of reading books together, discussing films, and analyzing texts. This cultural stratum becomes the basis for reflection and enrichment of one's own experience by trying on another's experience.

· Modern education is built on the principles of diversity, and home self-isolation is not a hindrance. Books and films, watching online concerts and virtual tours of museums, meditation (and even Friday's virtual gatherings on Skype or Zoom with friends and colleagues) will help. In order for this to be education, rather than entertainment, it is useful to keep a quarantine diary in which you can describe and analyze the new educational experience.

· The employer, by and large, is not so important as you grow wiser during the quarantine. The results of your work and contribution to solving the problems facing the company will be evaluated. Now most companies are forced to work in survival and self-preservation mode. The timing and consequences of quarantine are not clear. Obviously, you will have to adapt to new conditions, change business models, and principles of work. Although no one has a ready-made recipe for changes, several competencies and topics can be worked out in advance.

Learning new business models. You can see what companies from other industries or competitors make money on, first of all, digital companies. You need to carefully study the reports of companies, their presentations, reviews of consulting firms, lectures by business leaders - everything that will help to look at the activities of your company and your work in a different way. The coming months after quarantine is a developing situation with a zero budget, and solutions that allow achieving results with fewer resources will be appreciated. To understand and feel the philosophy of this approach, we recommend that you watch the movie "The Man Who Changed Everything" (Moneyball) - it is a must-see for all students of the Moscow School of Management Skolkovo.

Product and service development. Those companies that will be able to quickly introduce new products to the market will quickly emerge from the crisis. We need competencies to analyze consumer behavior and create the right customer experience, develop products, and scale production. Hundreds of available online courses will help you learn new competencies. You can study them in a month of intensive work.

Digital skills. In recent years, the so-called Hybrid competencies that combine traditional management and new digital skills (such as digital marketing or digital finance). Everything related to big data analysis and basic programming skills will be in demand. You can immerse yourself in the topic with the help of free courses at Coursera (for example, Data Science), which are jointly conducted by leading universities and technology companies.

We are very used to relying on the state or employers, but being in quarantine, we remain alone with ourselves. We have a good chance to critically evaluate our prospects and outline a concrete development plan for the next three months. In the early days, it will be important to pre-allocate time in your schedule for educational tasks and get into a rhythm: for example, three times a week for half an hour I study programming, two times an hour I study the best practices of other companies and listen to free webinars, every hour I meditate before bedtime. Right now, new competencies and principles of work are being laid, according to which the world will live in the future. And do not miss this opportunity.

14 ways to make money from home and round up your salary

Thousands of people are looking for work from home to round their wages every day.

If you, too, are ambitious and are looking around to earn more, if you are also looking for a way to round off by taking opportunities to carry on after work, today will give you 30 ideas to make money in your free time.

We will see together 14 different ways to earn and round the salary.

Fourteen chores from home that want to please everyone. In fact, I tried to select 30 opportunities, of which only some required specific skills and others that could be done by everyone or almost everyone. So not only by programmers, polyglots, etc...

Why are these topics so popular? Because we have entered what experts call GIG Economy. It means that we are in the economy of the integrative job done at home, where technology plays an important role. A part-time job that complements the salary and allows you to have more money at your disposal and beyond.

This is not the place to talk about how bad or good this is. Surely people are looking for more and more jobs that can supplement their salary. The statistics say it; it's a fact.

The reasons are many: the economic crisis, the increase in living costs, the perception of insecurity, the increasingly stressful jobs, the unbearable employers, the bad climate that you breathe in the company, and so on.

It does not happen only in Italy, in a study cited by Forbes magazine: By 2020, 50% of workers in the United States will supplement their wages with a home-based job.

These are incredible figures. Do you realize this?

There is nothing wrong with that. Indeed, 40% of companies expect to have many more GIG workers in the ranks of their employees; therefore, they are organizing themselves to create these opportunities and offer them to those who want to get involved and get busy in their free time.

Small but important premise: without work, without sweat on the forehead, without giving up, none of these ways produces fruit.

It should be superfluous to remember this, but it is not so. Maybe let's analyze the reasons again. Now let's move on to see all thirty opportunities because you are here for this.

To make life easier for everyone, at the end of each opportunity, I will tell you what I think by taking stock of the positive and negative aspects of that specific opportunity.

The 14 ways are as follows:

1. Risk-Free Betting

It is a question of betting with the money that cyclically online betting sites make available free of charge for those who register or those who involve friends by inviting them to register.

This is perhaps the easiest way to be able to have zero-cost money in your gaming account, without having to play your own capital.

Obviously, to be able to earn money, you have to play and win. It is clear that being able to sign up with various emails, being able to invite various friends, the possibility of being able to obtain interesting amounts rises.

PRO

- Real winnings where you risk someone else's money;
- vastness of sites and areas in which to specialize (sport, politics, events, shows ...)

VERSUS

- It takes a long time;
- can generate ludopathy;
- uncertain earnings (you make money only when you win, and if you win);
- reputation, and family peace issues.

2. Online surveys

Maybe you don't know it, but you can earn it by participating in market research and filling in the surveys that are paid to you.

Earnings are around 5 dollars gross per survey. Not even a little for the difficulty it takes to answer questions.

The areas are varied and range between many topics depending on the fashions of the moment: from the

evaluation of the products of the advertisements to the political orientation.

To participate in these market research, it usually takes from a few minutes to a few tens of minutes and is paid through Paypal in cash or with vouchers to spend in the main online stores (Amazon, online Supermarkets, etc.).

PRO

- Extreme simplicity;
- Certain earnings;
- Just a cell phone, even if the PC is more comfortable.

VERSUS

- Low earnings ($ 5 / survey);

- earnings related to the time you want to dedicate, non-scalable wealth without passive earnings;
- boring and repetitive work (often you get tired, before having earned the minimum threshold to get paid)

3. Online Trading

One of the most profitable but also more difficult activities to do to round off is to invest capital on the stock exchange and follow its trends, moving one's capital in order to earn more and more.

Today access to technologies for trading has become extremely simple, so much so that you do not need to have any technological knowledge. Just know the rules of trading.

To become a Wall-Street Wolf, a mobile phone is enough today, not to mention that in addition to the stock market, there is a promising crypto currency trading market to explore.

PRO

- Always accessible, just a mobile phone;
- Excellent for those with skills in the field, it allows earnings not related to time;
- Huge gains are possible with very little effort.

VERSUS

- Very high risks;
- Requires specific skills;
- Risk of scams in online training (difficult to have results with online courses);
- It requires cold blood and the ability to remain at a loss for long periods before earning.

4. Review Sites and Apps Online

User Testing pays you to browse a site and test an app.

 The review takes place by tracking your movements on the screen and recording your voice that comments on what it is seeing. As simple as drinking a glass of water. $ 10 is paid on PayPal for each 20-minute review. You will be given a checklist of actions to be performed, and you can give your opinion on that particular online service: a site or an app that has decided to let anonymous users evaluate its ease of use.

PRO

· Simple and affordable for many.

VERSUS

- The figures that can be earned are limited;
- The earnings mode is not scalable because it is linked to your free time;

- You earn if you know English to a level that can be understood when making reviews.

5. Kindle Publishing

Many dreams of writing the novel of life that will make them turn. What few people know is that you are able to write, you can publish your books on Amazon and earn from the thousands of people who will look for them online every day.

The Kindle is a device that is practically in all homes today, making books for Kindle has never been easier, and the earnings that can be made are truly remarkable.

The more languages you master, the more obvious business can become interesting. Especially when it comes to outsourcing the production of eBooks.

PRO

- You earn really important figures;

- activity unrelated to time is sold while sleeping;
- Secure and guaranteed payments.

VERSUS

- A business that totally depends on Amazon's policies is an extremely risky business (today there are certain conditions, but tomorrow these can change quickly);
- Complicated and laborious book-outsourcing;
- Requires an initial investment of around € 2,000 just to start seeing the first fruits.

6. Affiliate Marketing

Do you have a site that has a fair number of visitors or a social account with thousands of followers?

Then this is one of the most interesting activities to do in order to supplement the salary.

It involves redirecting your users or followers to a third-party site. If a sale takes place on this third site, you can take a commission.

The provision varies from about 1% to 70%; it depends very much on the cases and the markets in which you decide to operate, in any case, it is a very interesting activity, even if it is not easy to bring it up to speed.

PRO

- Interesting figures are earned, and they are not independent of the weather; therefore, one also earns while sleeping;
- Opportunity to work on your interests;
- You monetize a digital property that you already have (website visited, account with many followers).

VERSUS

- The English language is the one that guarantees the most interesting earnings;
- Digital marketing and site development skills that not everyone has been useful;
- Difficult to orientate in the choice of partners;
- Constant work is needed to maintain income.

7. Sale or resale of used items

One of the easiest activities to do if you want to raise some money to round off is to free the attics of the objects that we no longer use, but that can still be used by others.

We immediately think of books, gym equipment, but not only. On sites similar to eBay, Craigslist, and even on Face book, you can find items for sale at, particularly affordable prices.

These items can be purchased and then resold at a higher price. In fact, it often happens that the owners do not know the true value of some used books or certain comics that came out about thirty years ago. And this can be used to our advantage.

PRO

- Simple activity;
- Good margins,
- Ecological, an activity that goes against the culture of waste.

VERSUS

- Time-related activity, non-scalable;
- Expensive, when the time to constantly look for new products to resell increased is a demanding activity.

8. Buying and selling of web domains

A domain name is not just a web address. Sometimes domain dominates the brand value; other times, it makes you easily remembered or found on search engines.

Therefore the value of a domain often exceeds the average cost of 9 euros for the annual renewal. In fact, in 2007, the VacationRentals.com domain was auctioned for a considerable amount of 35 million dollars.

Maybe you don't know it, but there are dozens of services that help you sell the domains you have registered and that you don't use, making you monetize what has so far been only a cost. One of these platforms is Sedo.com, but there are many others.

PRO

· You earn certain and get paid immediately.

VERSUS

- Difficult to start from scratch today;

- The best earnings are obtained on the international market; therefore, it is advisable to know the languages;
- Trading interesting domains requires substantial capital.

9. Making the Appearance

Making an appearance in a film is certainly not a job, a very difficult activity, but it is well paid. It is done where you turn, and you follow the indications of who is filming.

But it is an often-paid job that can also reserve some emotions, especially when some famous actors become approachable for a greeting or for a small conversation.

A film appearance takes around € 100 a day, but there are also paid extras on talk shows and television programs that require an audience.

PRO

· You earn certain and get paid immediately.

VERSUS

- It is necessary to live near the film studios in which you turn;
- It is a leisure-time activity that cannot be scaled in any way.

10. Selling Online Courses (info-products)

If you think you can do something and if you believe there are people willing to buy your knowledge so that you can teach them what you know, this is perhaps one of the best opportunities you have to round off if not really to achieve economic freedom.

Often we don't feel adequate, but every student who knows less than us about a topic perceives us as experts. Therefore, all people who know less than us can be helped by our knowledge.

So the business of info products is one of the most profitable that can be done today. So much so that not infrequently, those who start their work shortly afterward to dedicate themselves only to that.

PRO

- Earnings certain and paid in advance;
- Up-sell possibility on consultancy;
- Scalable earnings unrelated to time.

VERSUS

- It is necessary to have transversal skills (digital marketing, video editing, web development, community management)
- The equipment to leave can be very expensive. Even if you record with a mobile phone, the software to assemble, the PC with a memory capable of managing videos, the cost of advertising are all variables capable of complicating things a lot even for the most expert.

11. Sell photos

The images are essential to promote our products and to accompany our online stories. For this, there are numerous portals that sell photographs to those who need to accompany the content with a visual part to support it.

This is an excellent earning opportunity because you just need to download the contract with these portals where the specifications of the photos are dictated and follow the instructions to make the shots.

In fact, it is a sale of copyrights brokered by a web portal that finds the customers who need the photos for you.

PRO

- Certain earnings;
- Scalable earnings unrelated to time;
- Possibility to combine work with a hobby.

VERSUS

- Low marginality for a single photo;

- Brokerage commissions that cut the margin considerably.

12. YouTube

YouTube is one of the very few platforms that reward creative's who make money out of it. Little or a lot, this is not the point, but today YouTube is one of the very few social networks that pay to upload something on it. From here, many have managed to make a fortune that starts with the first thousands of euros made with advertising and ends by adding sponsorships, product placements, appearances, and so on.

PRO

- Interesting earnings;
- Earnings disconnected at the time.

VERSUS

- Expensive equipment to make really good videos;

- To maintain the annuity, it is not possible to stop working and always produce new videos
- The creation of a well-made video can take many hours of time;
- Statistically few earn much, while very many make only a few cents a month.

13. Reconversion Crowd funding

It's called Reconversion Crowd funding, and it's the way you can earn by paying a share for the redevelopment of a property. All this takes place through special platforms that can manage and accompany you throughout the entire process.

They are platforms very similar to crowd funding platforms (Kick starter, IndieGoGo, etc.) but specialized in the real estate world.

On average, projects of this type are able to yield about 9% per year.

PRO

- Interesting earnings;
- No technical knowledge required;
- Earnings disconnected from time.

VERSUS

· The need for capital to invest.

14. Ghostwriter & Copywriter

How many entrepreneurs are thinking of writing a book for personal branding? Lots! Too bad, they don't know where to start. If you can write well and think you are able to prepare books for third parties, this is a great business opportunity for you.

Likewise, many entrepreneurs are looking for people who write for their content, brochures, corporate blog posts.

The key part of this activity is to get started and let word of mouth do its job.

PRO

- Writing a book for a corporate manager can yield excellent earnings;

- The activity offers opportunities for relationships with people who then move on to other jobs.

VERSUS

- Opportunity linked to the time dedicated to writing and promoting your business;
- Non-scalable activity;
- It requires not only writing skills but in-depth knowledge of the topics on which you want to write

21 creative (and educational) ideas to do with kids at home

We have started an exceptional period of confinement in houses as a containment measure to deal with the pandemic virus. Today we propose 21 creative and educational ideas to do with children at home.

These days will be a great challenge for family life, but they can also be a great opportunity. We take the opportunity to co-responsibility children by promoting their participation in the organization of schedules and family routines. It is important to keep them as much as possible, although you will have to be flexible and have a great deal of patience and empathy. A useful and participatory strategy may be to create a calendar with drawings and time slots to establish what time we will spend on household chores, school chores, playing games, working (in the case of adults who can telework), sleeping, to the screens, etc. In this section, you will find more general tips to organize yourself.

In addition, we believe that it is essential to stimulate free play as long as possible since it is from this that children grow and develop more naturally and healthily. A good way to stimulate free play is to have the play spaces ready, perhaps for different corners of activity, and to put relaxing ambient music to help the fluency of the game and the concentration of the children.

Apart from these general premises, here are our 21 creative ideas for activities, games, and experiments to make them a fun day with plenty of opportunities to learn, grow, and live in good humor:

1. Make crafts

The moments to create can be very enriching for boys and girls to develop their creativity, fine motor skills, patience, and tranquility. Crafts have many benefits. Depending on the age of the children, some techniques will be more suitable than others. It is important to keep in mind that these should be moments of little directed crafts, appealing to the creative and expression freedom of children and letting them experiment with materials without fear. And, as mothers and fathers, try not to restrict ourselves too much because of the fear that they will get dirty... we will have to clean each other when the activity is over.

Different strategies can be proposed: o (1) we prepare a wardrobe, drawer or box with all the necessary materials for various crafts and that the children explore all the possibilities, or (2) we start with an initial material and each day we provide a material new in the box. In this way, we are dosing the creative possibilities.

We can use materials or techniques such as mandalas, finger paints, tempera, watercolors, chalk, pastel colors, modeling clay, moldable wax, clay, origami, glitter, stickers and washi tape, bracelets with embroidery threads, wool, recycled materials, puppets with socks, painting stones, making mobiles with woods ... imagination and creativity to power!

2. Photo albums

We can commission older children to prepare these photo albums these days that we have wanted to do for a long time and never find the time... to select the images, print them, paste them in a notebook, and make comments... or else in digital format. So, they also train their digital skills. With the youngest and youngest, we can prepare memory board games at home with photos of family or close friends.

3. Read stories, books, and comics

We dust in the home library and encourage the reading of illustrated stories, comics, or books. If those of us at home have already read them many times, we try to make some exchange with friends or neighbors, always avoiding crowds, according to health recommendations. We can also search for the *e-book* in digital format, or buy one online.

We can also search for audio books in mp3, Spanish, or English on Spotify or other online audio book platforms. Listening to stories without seeing the images helps to develop children's imagination and inner wealth.

4. Lots of music

We take advantage of these homemade days so that boys and girls enjoy music. We listen to the music of all kinds, we sing together, we play improvised instruments, we make room in the living room to dance. Children love to share moments of dance and body expression with adults, and we must bear in mind that throughout the day, we will have to combine moments of more active and physically intense activities with calmer moments. Dancing and music are a good opportunity.

Have you played the chained songs game? You can start practicing as a family; you'll see how much fun!

5. We share hobbies or hobbies

If you like sewing, crocheting, DIY, modeling, giant puzzles, or you have other hobbies that can be done indoors, maybe it is time to share them with your sons and daughters, and they can start practicing on their own. Take into account their age and assess whether they are adapted activities that they can do with some autonomy and safely.

6. A bit of video games or screens

During the day, there will be moments for everything. We have to agree on some schedules or screen times depending on age (including video games, mobiles, tablets, cartoons, television). With younger children who still cannot read the time on a watch, we recommend using an hourglass to make it more visual and clearer as time goes by. We must take into account the experts' recommendations such as Serge Tisseron's 3-6-9-12 rule.

The WHO in 2019 makes recommendations regarding the use of screens in childhood that say that children under 2-3 years of age should not use the screens or watch TV and that from 2 years of age at most one hour a day. But in addition to screen time, we will have to control the quality of what they see or what they play with: that there is no violent, sexist, or racist content and that it is appropriate to the age of the children.

7. Board games

Board games are very interesting to delve into various skills and abilities. We especially recommend cooperative board games because they propose a collective challenge and favor play without violence or competitiveness. Board games in general and especially cooperative games are a great educational tool to promote teamwork and skills such as concentration, strategy, etc.

8. Cooking as a family

Cooking as a family is very fun and enriching. It stimulates learning and coexistence. If we can, we take advantage of these days to make all kinds of recipes with children: salads, fruit salads, cookies, cakes, etc. And from 8-10 years old, they can start to cook on their own simple and safe recipes. These days that boys and girls will spend many hours at home, they can be the chefs of the family, right?

From cooking and recipes, children can train creativity and many abilities and skills such as reading, writing, mathematics, volumes, weights, fine motor skills, we can train ourselves in home cooking techniques, by making yogurts knead bread or sprout seeds for salads.

9. Movement or group games

These games are suitable for large families or for adults and children to play together. Every day we must stimulate movement games even if it is inside the house. You can search for ideas in our resource bank or follow these examples:

- Hide for rooms
- The darkroom
- The game of the movies
- Hide objects or toys for the house and play "hot or cold."
- Worm racing, upside down, down the hall
- The set of cooperative chairs
- Pica wall
- The twister

10. Make cabins inside the house

Who hasn't dreamed of a cabin in their living room when they were little? Kids love the cabins! We can help them build them and then let them play calmly and let their imaginations run wild, or if they are quite autonomous, we prepare the material for them, and they can build it themselves.

We can use sofas, chairs, tables, blankets, beds, sheets, cardboard boxes; the possibilities are endless and the game and the fun too!

11. Propose a challenge every day

We can propose a daily challenge and even pose it as a calendar of surprises in which every morning we discover the challenge. Some of the challenges could be (depending on age):

- Do any of the activities mentioned above.
- Prepare a homemade gift for grandparents and grandmothers or other relatives.
- Make a very high tower with all the construction pieces that we have around the house until we get to touch the roof.
- Line up chained socks on the floor, how many meters will it be long?
- Write a letter or draw a picture for a friend from school (and mail it to them!).
- Make up a song with fun lyrics that talk about our family.
- Sort toys and choose the ones we don't use to give or sell second-hand.
- Count how many blue objects are in the whole house.
-

12. Do yoga, meditation, and relaxation

Practicing yoga has many benefits for children: it improves concentration, learning, attention, self-knowledge, control of breathing, relaxation, balance, etc. During these days, there may be times where boys and girls can practice yoga or meditation. A mat and some useful guides are enough. Do you know the Eduioga game? A good combination of yoga and card games. Here you can see a demonstration of yoga for children.

13. Communicate with friends

We must keep in mind that for our sons and daughters, friendships are very important. The fact that the school is closed and those collective activities are limited for a few days can make children feel more alone or insecure, and that their social interactions are weakened.

We can take advantage of WhatsApp contacts with other families to exchange videos, audios, and images of the activities we do. Surely we can share ideas and promote friendship ties. From 10 years old, we can practice video conferences through different platforms and 3 or 4 bands to promote digital and communication skills.

14. Housework

These days at home can also be a good opportunity to consolidate habits or involve children in aspects of daily life and household chores. Apart from cooking, there are many other tasks that can make them feel very useful and responsible. Just as in the colonies, we dedicate time to what we call "services," at home, we can also establish criteria for who is responsible for each task. Depending on their age, they can be responsible for: setting and removing the table, setting the dishwasher, washing dishes manually, setting the washing machine, hanging clothes, sweeping, scrubbing, cleaning the windows, dusting, storing clothes wardrobe, etc.

15. The costume chest

We can organize a box, trunk, or wardrobe with costumes of all types and sizes for you to experiment with. We can add adult clothing and accessories - kids love that their clothes go big! Hats, caps, scarves, belts, necklaces, shoes, fabrics of different sizes, and colors ... anything goes! Imagination to the power!

If we put the costume chest near a mirror and also provide face paints, it will be even more fun!

16. Marble circuits

The marble or ball circuits stimulate the development of creativity and imagination, as well as favoring concentration, patience, spatial organization, and the development of mathematical and physical thought. In addition, they help train fine motor skills and hand-eye coordination. Currently, there are many commercial brands of toys that have ball circuits. We recommend only those that are made of wood or recycled materials.

But we encourage you to help your sons and daughters create homemade marble circuits and have a good time creating and then using them.

17. Other creations with recycled material

We can use all kinds of recycled materials; cardboard boxes of all sizes, newspapers, clean tetra bricks, bottles, plastic caps, etc.

to build objects, toys, or inventions. For example, make a boat, a castle, a farm, a cabin, a tower, a tadpole, a mask, a car, a rocket, juggling balls, etc. We use our imagination, and from recycled materials and a little paint and glue, we can create to infinity.

18. Scientific experiments

Children can practice scientific inventions at home under the supervision of adults. From more or less simple experiences, adapted to the age of the children, they can discover and practice basic principles of chemistry, physics, biology, geology, mathematics, have you not tried to make a volcano with vinegar and bland? Or experiment with sound by making a phone with yogurt cans? Or plant legumes in damp cotton to germinate?

19. Games in the bathtub

Up to 8-9 years old playing and experimenting in the bathtub can be very stimulating and fun. In the case of young children, we must be extremely vigilant when bathing. But these days, we can appeal to our creativity and invent original baths with bubbles, or water dyed with colors with food coloring, or with background music, or with dolls and boats to play a symbolic game. Attention, but watch the water consumption and do not fill the bathtubs too much or too often.

20. Make theater

In some corners of the house, we can set up an improvised stage, hang a curtain, and encourage children to do plays and develop their stage skills. We can also set up a puppet theater and make finger puppets and have them make up stories. Older boys and girls can prepare good script, decoration material, costumes, makeup, music, etc.

Another option is to make theater with Chinese shadows; first we will have to cut out the shapes on the cardboard, prepare the sheet, and go ahead with creativity to invent good work.

21. Practice creative writing

These days give a lot to write ... the stories that are emerging and that we can imagine as a result of the exceptional situation we are experiencing. We can take advantage of it to awaken our creativity and start writing. We will have to take into account the age of the children and combine drawing with writing. Writing or making up stories is a good way to channel emotions, stress, anguish, and also awaken humor and a critical spirit.

What can we write?

- A diary of each day of the confinement: we can stick photos or make drawings of everything we are doing and (depending on the age) of the news of the day of the pandemic follow-up.
- Letters to the people we love, especially the grandparents who are alone at home or confined in residences, then we can take a photo to send by WhatsApp.
- Fictional stories we make up; With children under 6 we can create illustrated albums without lyrics or with little lyrics.
- Comics.
- The chain story game: one person writes a sentence, folds the paper, and leaves only one or two words in sight, from which the other person has to continue the story. Then the second person folds again and leaves only one

word in sight, and so on. It will be a crazy story!

How to Make Homemade Hand Sanitizer after Supermarket Stocks Run Out

The pandemic virus is causing " panic," and the first thing that has become exhausted and more expensive is masks and hand sanitizers.

The worldwide outbreak of the pandemic virus has sparked widespread fear that has led to the exhaustion of face masks and **hand sanitizers** in supermarkets.

Hence, see options to prevent without the need to spend that money.

Any prevention mechanism at this time is little, especially the main recommendation: wash your hands as **many times as possible.** Do not cut yourself when going to wash your hands either before meals, after going to the bathroom, after contact with partner objects, after using public transport viruses and batteries are everywhere and in this At this time, when the pandemic virus is not detected immediately, prevention must still be greater.

As experts have reported: "There are a large number of microorganisms present in our day to day, from which effect we can protect ourselves if we wash our hands about six times a day." There are also **more than 200 diseases from which contagion can be escaped if we maintain this hygienic**

custom. Including that dreaded pandemic virus that, at the moment, fills countries like Italy and Spain with concern.

Hand sanitizing gel can be made at home

The situation is so critical that, as we say, the stocks of **hydro alcoholic** hand **gel** are **depleted almost everywhere**, and the few that remain are very expensive.

This solution can also be very useful to us, beyond conventional soap. The addition of being able to make it on our own at home makes it even more attractive.

How do we make hand sanitizing gel at home?

The **ingredients** for this homemade hydro alcoholic gel, extrapolated for approximately one liter, would be the following:

· 833 ml of 96 or 99% alcohol

· 42 ml of hydrogen peroxide

· 15 ml of glycerin (glycerol 98%)

You have to **mix everything well** and, very importantly, **let the liquid sit for at least 72 hours before using it**. Once that period of time has been exceeded, we will have our homemade hydro alcoholic gel. We already know: **prevention is better than cure**. And more in these times of alarm, and even some psychosis, before diseases such as the pandemic virus.

Tips to properly clean and disinfect your home against the pandemic virus

During the period of isolation, it is necessary that you avoid all risks and implement strict hygiene measures

At the **current juncture**, it is vitally important to take hygienic precautions in order to avoid infections, because the new virus is an extremely contagious virus. Not only do they warn about the **importance of washing hands** in order to fight the disease, but they also insist (naturally) on cleaning objects that **come into contact** with patients, since it is unknown how long **the pandemic virus survives** in a surface but could be hours or even days, according to some studies.

So perhaps the measures that **South Korea was** taking a month ago, fumigating the **evacuees from Wuhan, are** no longer so **striking**. If at this time we have to spend a lot of time at home **due to isolation**, it is logical that we take extreme precautions in our home in order not to get infected or, if there is a family member who is already sick, that it does not spread further.

The patient

The Ministry of Health recommends that you stay in your room, that it be ventilated, and if possible, with the door closed. You should also avoid distances of less than two meters with the people you live with, no visitors, and **have a hand hygiene product and a garbage can** inside the room. It would also be a good idea to have a personal bathroom, if possible.

How to do it

The rest of the inhabitants of the house, of course, must **take extreme precautions.**

In the kitchen, use the dishwasher whenever you can and, if you don't have it, scrub with hot water. Of course, don't share **any utensils.**

In the bathroom, clean it (also the toilet) with disposable cloths and bleach. Ammonia is also a good option. Both in this part of the house and in the kitchen, precautions must be taken.

The patient must remain in his room with the door closed and a garbage can. If possible, you should use a bathroom exclusively for him

In the living room and bedrooms, if your sofa has a cover, the best thing you can do is remove it to disinfect it. Clean the windows inside and out, and don't shake your clothes. Also, try to wash curtains and any other textiles that can be cleaned, such as pillowcases or towels, as well as cabinets inside. Wash the patient's clothes in a separate laundry.

Wear a **mask and gloves** to clean the house.

Cleaning is not disinfecting.

The problem with this virus is that it is new and, therefore, we have very little information about it. Since we don't really know how long it survives on surfaces, fear is greater. As journalist **Sarah Zhang points out** in ' **The Atlantic** ': "Up until a few weeks ago, cleanliness meant only dusting a little and making the bed. Then the pandemic virus came, and everything changed. First, the schools closed and then the work, and now it seems that, because of fear, there is an awareness of the matter. "

The journalist also stresses that, in times of this pandemic, it is essential to disinfect doorknobs, handrails, keyboards, etc., everything that is touched frequently. In case you have doubts about **the difference between cleaning and disinfecting**, the first refers only to the use of soap and water to eliminate dirt and most germs. **Disinfection**, by contrast, refers to the use of cleaning solutions that contain ingredients that kill bacteria and other germs.

Therefore, without getting paranoid, it is best to **clean (and disinfect)** the house several times a day, especially those parts most susceptible to harboring the virus and **remember to** always **wash your hands** when finished and leave the cleaning products to work the time required, reading the labels beforehand to know their use.

Mask against the pandemic virus. Do you really need it?

Because of recent news, **we have seen an unnecessary increase in the use of face masks in our immediate environment.** There are shortages, and those who really need them (a person with immunodeficiency, for example) have trouble getting them.

As there are some confusion and a lot of over-information, we want to explain, as we have said before, only in the case that it is strictly necessary, the different types that

243

exist, and their use in a hospital environment. But before entering the matter, it is **IMPORTANT** that you first watch this video, in which we explain the appropriate hygienic measures to avoid the spread of the pandemic virus.

Do you know what the main types of masks are?

On the one hand, we have a **surgical mask**, which is what we see in clinical settings. It aims to protect the patient from possible contamination by healthcare personnel, and that the exhaled air is filtered as much as possible to avoid contaminating the people around us.

As it is not designed to filter inhaled air, it cannot be considered PPE (Personal Protective Equipment, according to Royal Decree 773/1997), because it does not seek to filter the air we breathe, but to filter the air we expel during breathing when coughing or sneezing.

It is classified by its efficiency in bacterial filtration (type I: <= 95% and type II: <= 98%) and the pressure of resistance to splashes (type R: <= 120 mm Hg), which would protect against the screening of biological fluids (e.g., blood).

On the other hand, **the mask that is PPE** (personal protective equipment) meets other control requirements and regulations (Royal Decree 1407/2009), because its purpose is to filter the inhaled air, preventing contaminants from entering our respiratory system.

The most similar to the surgical mask is the FFP (Filtering *Face Piece*) self-filtering mask, capable of filtering particles and aerosols (micro droplets).

PROTECTION CLASS	% RETENTION	Nominal Protection Factor
FFP1	78%	4
FFP2	92%	12
FFP3	98%	50

UNE-EN 149 FPN standard = 100 /% Leak

To better understand this table, download the guide for the selection of respiratory protection equipment.

How can we check the correct fit of the mask?

It is important that the mask is appropriate for the risk against which we protect ourselves, and that it adjusts to our physical characteristics. It must be appropriate to our physiognomy, to our face, and it must fit perfectly to prevent air that may be contaminated from passing between our face and mask, avoiding filter material that would prevent us from being exposed to risk.

It is very important to raise awareness about checking for a good fit on the mask, because **if it does not fit well it does not protect**. We must therefore be able to sensitize those responsible or managers to take into account:

- The level of protection of the person based on their physical characteristics.
- The selection of the equipment that best suits the user in terms of sizes and models.
- The importance of a correct fit through a fit test

The adjustment methods that we know:

- **Qualitative method:** The worker will be exposed to a certain product (notably saccharin or Bittrex), and is based on the user's senses.
- **Quantitative method**: using a quantitative method, we will measure the possible leaks of the equipment.

Both methods check the fit by performing 7 exercises of one minute each, which are:

- Breathe normally.
- Breathe deeply.
- Shake your head from side to side.
- Move your head up and down.
- Read or speak aloud.
- Flex the body at the waist.
- Breathe normally again.

Taking into account that the qualitative method depends on the perceptions of the individual, it is preferable to always be able to perform the test using a quantitative method.

The purpose of the surgical mask, due to its design, is adequate to prevent the wearer from contaminating the environment. Its tissue collects the microdroplets that we can exhale when breathing, but it is more difficult for it to retain all the particles in the environment when we inhale, since it does not seal its perimeter.

Masks that are PPE must meet specific requirements to avoid inhaling contaminants (in this case dust and micro droplets). And on many occasions, they are designed with exhalation valves to promote breathing and remove heat from our breath. There are also some masks that meet the two standards and allow their use as PPE and as a sanitary mask (these do not have an exhalation valve).

In conclusion, hospitals use:

- Surgical masks for those infected or who may be, to avoid infecting other people.
- FFP2 or FFP3 self-filtering masks for healthy personnel who may be in contact with or who may be infected, to avoid becoming infected.
- FFP3 self-filtering masks, for healthcare personnel who perform aerosol-generating procedures with patients, such as tracheal intubation, tracheostomy, cardiopulmonary resuscitation, etc.

These measures should ALWAYS be accompanied by others such as hand washing, etc.

Uses of cloth face masks to help delay the spread of the new virus.

The Center of Disease Control of the United States has just recommended the use of face masks to delay the progress of the infection. In Spain the Ministry of Health is studying to introduce its compulsory use in public spaces. According to the director general of the Chinese Center for Disease Control and Prevention, George Gao: "The big mistake in the United States and Europe, in my opinion, is that people don't wear face masks. This virus is transmitted by droplets and close contact. The drops play a very important role: you have to wear a mask, because when you speak, drops always come out of your mouth, hesays "Many people have asymptomatic or presymptomatic infections". By wearing face masks, you can prevent the virus-carrying drops from escaping and infecting others."

The masks must:

- Fit snugly yet comfortably on the face surface.
- Secure with ties or gums to the ears.
- Include multiple layers of fabric.
- Allow unrestricted breathing.
- Able to machine wash and dry without damaging or losing shape.

CDC Recommendations for Homemade Facial Covers.

The CDC recommends using cloth face masks in public places where other measures of social distancing are difficult to maintain (Example, supermarkets and pharmacies), especially in areas of significant community transmission.

The CDC also recommends the use of cloth face masks to delay the spread of the virus and to prevent people who may have the virus and not know it from passing it on to others.

Cloth face masks made from household items or made from common materials can be used as an additional voluntary public health measure.

Cloth face masks should not be placed on children under 2 years of age, anyone who is having trouble breathing, or is unconscious, disabled, or unable to remove the mask without assistance.

The recommended cloth masks are not surgical masks or N-95 respirators. Those are supplies that should continue to be reserved for healthcare workers and other first responders, as recommended by current CDC guidance.

Should face cloth covers be washed or cleaned regularly? How often?

Yes. They should be washed routinely depending on the frequency of use.

How do I safely sterilize / clean a fabric face covering?

A washing machine is enough to properly wash a face covering.

You can also heat water to 60C and leave them with soap and water for a few minutes. Rinse and dry in the sun or in the dryer.

How do you safely remove a used face mask?

People should be careful not to touch their eyes, nose and mouth when removing the face covering and wash their hands with soap immediately after removing them.

Materials to make a fabric mask with a sewing machine

• Two rectangles of cotton fabric 25 cm x 15 cm

• Two 15 cm elastic pieces (or rubber bands, strings, cloth strips or hair bands)

• Needle and thread (or hairpin)

• Scissors

• Sewing machine

1. Cut out two rectangles of 25 by 15 cm cotton cloth. Use dense cotton, such as quilted fabrics or cotton sheets. The fabric of a T-shirt is worth it if necessary. Stack the two rectangles; sew the mask as if it were a single piece of cloth.

2. Fold over the long sides 0.5 cm and make the hem. Then fold the double layer of fabric about 1 cm along the short sides and sew down.

3. Pass about 15 cm of elastic band about 0.5 cm wide through the widest edge on each side of the mask. These will be the ear muffs. Use a large needle or hairpin to pass it. Tie the ends well. Do not have elastic? Use headbands or elastic headbands. If you only have a rope, or hair ties, you can make the longest ties and tie the mask behind your head.

4. Pull the elastic so that the knots are tucked inside the hem. Adjust the sides of the mask with the elastic so that the mask fits your face. Then securely sew the elastic in place to prevent slipping.

Mask made with a T-shirt (without sewing machine)

Materials

Shirt

Scissors

7-8 inches approximately 17-20 cm

6-7 inches approximately 15-17 cm

Mask made with a scarf

Materials used:

Handkerchief (or cotton square fabric about 50 x50 cm)

Coffee filter

Rubber bands (or hair bands)

Scissors (if you are cutting your own fabric)

- Fold the filter in the center of the scarf. Fold the top down. Fold the bottom up.
- Place chicken gums or hair gums 15 cm from each
- Fold the side towards the center and fold it

What is the best mask to prevent the pandemic virus?

A new virus of animal origin is in full swing. It is the virus known as **pandemic virus** or **Wuhan's virus**; referring to the Chinese city where it first appeared caused by a new virus of animal origin that is in full swing.

In this situation, a state of alarm is taking place in public opinion that causes many people, companies and entities to acquire respiratory protection equipment for protection against this virus. There are multiple types of masks and each one offers a very different degree of protection against the 2019-nCoV virus.

What pandemic virus mask to buy?

Before acquiring a mask, it is necessary to know the different types of **respiratory protection products** available and to be very clear about the most valid to protect yourself against this disease in the most effective way possible.

The level of classification is essential to guarantee the safety of the users who wear the masks. We can speak of two types:

Depending on whether or not they have a valve with filter and the protection index.

Within the protection there are three categories according to their minimum filtration (78%, 92% and 98%, respectively).

Filtering degree of the masks:

- **FF P1**: they offer a minimum filtering efficiency of around 78%. The filtering power is also measured with the concept of Total leakage towards the interior, which in this case has a maximum admissible value of 22%
- **FF P2**: offer a minimum filtering efficiency of around 92% (maximum total leak rate of 8%).
- **FF P3**: offer a minimum filtering efficiency of around 98% (maximum total leak rate of 2%).

In addition, the masks are classified as non-reusable (NR) and reusable (R). Non-reusable equipment is to be used only during a work shift.

Although there is no unanimity among experts on the level of protection against this type of threat. While some speak of a FFP2, others go to the highest protection index and opt for FFP3.

The **Organization World of the Health** (**WHO**) recommends the use of masks with a filtration efficiency of at the least 95% for particles of 0.3 microns in diameter or more before isolation procedures or possible generation of infectious aerosols (measles, tuberculosis, SARS ...).

In summary, **these masks, called N95, are at a level of protection between FFP2 and FFP3**.

The masks that offer you the most security are those that have an FFP3 or N95 classification, since they retain smaller particles.

In addition, the appropriate size must be chosen so that the mask fits perfectly on the face of the user. Only then can complete security be provided.

That is why the ideal is to check the tight and tight fit with each use in order to eliminate leaks and follow the installation instructions to verify the correct sealing, in case of doubts.

- The adjustment system. Check that your mask has an ergonomic shape and that it fits properly to your face. Do not buy those that allow air to enter through the edges.
- The fastening system: Make sure you buy the right mask size for you. The best models have elastic or adjustable bands for a more comfortable and faster placement.

- The vent valves. Ideally, your mask offers a valve that allows adequate exhalation of warm, moist air. This allows for greater durability, prevents condensation of water inside the mask, reduces fogging of the lenses and gives you greater comfort.

Regardless of the effectiveness of the masks, their usefulness plummets if they are not well adjusted on the face, if they are turned inside out (with the white part facing out) or if they are reused in the case of surgical masks. All of these bad practices have been observed frequently among mask wearers.

The mask is always an additional protection measure. You must learn to follow best practices on how to put them on, take them off, and dispose of them. Precautions should also be taken regarding hand hygiene measures after removal.

Standard surgical masks **are designed to block large particles. They are not intended for tiny virus particles,** and are often baggy with spaces around the nose, mouth, and chin. This means that they are not effective against the virus.

Physical activity at the time of the new virus

A series of indications and advice on how to keep active during the epidemic are as follows:

The **pandemic** virus can make it difficult to maintain a physically active lifestyle, but we try with this section to give you some ideas and suggestions.

Based on what we know so far about the new virus, this virus appears to have **very high transmissibility potential**. This is why the ministerial provisions and recommendations are all aimed at avoiding contact with others as much as possible and, if this is necessary, at keeping us at a social distance of at least 1 meter from each other.

These measures obviously have contraindications, and one of these is the difficulty of **carrying out the physical activity**: gyms and fitness centers, as well as city parks, are closed. The traditional *corset* is also *prohibited* unless this takes place in the immediate vicinity of our home. In this period of generalized quarantine, therefore, it is almost inevitable to remain many hours **sitting and inactive**.

What can we do about it?

We start from the indications of the *World Health Organization* (WHO), which even in *normal* times recommends dedicating **at least 20 minutes a day to physical**

activity: international guidelines, in fact, identify in 150-300 minutes a week the amount of optimal physical activity to maintain a healthy and correct lifestyle.

Note well that we talk about **lifestyle** in general, precisely because carrying out an adequate and constant physical activity not only affects the much-feared *bacon* but also has countless other benefits for our whole body. Regular physical activity, in addition to making us lose weight by eliminating those extra *pounds*, also helps us to:

Increase the body's **immune defenses** and consequently decrease the chances of contracting viruses and diseases

Reduce stress and anxiety, which is a period like the one we are experiencing have certainly increased

Improve sleep quality and consequently our psycho-physical well-being

Once the ideal physical activity *requirement has been* established, we must understand how we can pursue this goal with all the limitations to which we are subject.

The pandemic virus, ten exercises to do to train at home during the quarantine

Among the measures taken by the government to contain the spread of the pandemic virus, there is also the closing of gyms. A piece of news that made the most fanatics of sport and fitness angry and cheered those who in that weight room were obliged to do so by a monthly charge on their checking account. But it's good news, because in isolation, your home can become the perfect place to continue training or where to start doing it for those who always postpone the fateful registration in the gym until next Monday.

With so much time available, there are many activities that can be done within the home and many exercises to keep you fit despite the appeal of the sofa and the long list of backward TV series. So here is a circuit of ten exercises to continue training in the inexhaustible hours you spend at home. You will need a mat or a common carpet. An elastic band, a sofa, and lots of goodwill.

1. Bend over sofa (10)

Start with the pushups. Just turn your relaxation sofa into useful gym equipment. Place your hands on the sofa so that you have less weight off the arms. Place your hands at a distance from each other equal to the width of your shoulders or slightly wider. Try to go down slowly and touch the sofa with your chest and then return to the starting position, always trying to keep the pelvis retroversion.

2. Elastic Pull (10)

Sitting comfortably on your carpet or mat, take a rubber band and fix it under your feet. If you want to get more tension, spread your feet apart. While adjusting the resistance roll, the elastic in your hand, the more it will be rolled up, the more you will struggle. Pull the elastic towards you with your elbows attached to your body. I recommend shoulders down and straight back, do not arch forward. Then take the elastic back to its original position without ever losing control.

3. Barchetta (30s)

For lovers of fitness and the gym, this is certainly one of the most feared exercises, but also among the most effective for those who want to get a steel abdomen. Classic isometric exercise to train all the abdominal muscles. From a belly-up position, we raise the legs and stretch our arms in front of us (simplified version) and hold the position going to form a boat. For the more adventurous, you can bring your arms straight behind the back of the neck. We maintain the position without losing tension or control of the pelvis, which must be reversed for the duration of the exercise.

4. Plank (30s)

Another resistance exercise is highly effective for training the whole body. On your stomach, rest your forearms on the floor in a straight line with your shoulders so that they are parallel to each other. Lift your buttocks, but please, don't keep them too high. I hold the position for 30 seconds. Remember to breathe.

5. Side plank (30s)

Same exercise, but this time goes to strengthen the oblique abs and the transverse muscle of the abdomen. Always free body positions yourself on your side and rest your elbow on the ground and then lift yourself off the floor. The whole body weight is concentrated on the forearm, which also, in this case, must remain in line with the shoulder.

6. Hyperextensions (30s)

Position yourself lying on the ground with your stomach on the floor (prone position); your legs stretched with your feet hammered. The hands can be placed behind the nape, under the chin, along the sides with the palms of the hand upwards, stretched forward. Hold the position for 30 seconds.

7. Ground bridges (30s)

Lie on your back (belly up), stretch your arms at your sides, bend your knees, rest your feet on the ground and then lift both the buttocks and the pelvis while always maintaining the upper back, shoulders, arms, and head lean on the floor. Raise and hold the position for 30 seconds.

8. Wall chair (30s)

Since all you need for this exercise is a wall, the walls of your home will be perfect. Position your shoulders against the wall, lean your back firmly on it and imagine an imaginary chair. Position your feet at equal distances to your femur from the wall, trying to obtain an angle of approximately 90 degrees. Place your head against the wall and keep your hands at your sides. Hold the position for 30 seconds.

9. Jumping jack (10)

You thought you could get by without cardio? Yes, many parks are closed as well as gyms, but there are exercises at home that can help your aerobic training. Feet united with legs extended and arms at your sides, raise your arms above your head and jump spreading your legs. Always in sync, return to the starting position and continue to repeat the movement without stopping.

10. Elastic stretches (10)

An excellent shoulder exercise is a military press. Standing, pass the elastic under the feet spaced apart shoulder-width apart. Once again, hold the elastic and bring your hands to shoulder height. With your back straight push upwards until your elbow is almost completely extended, check the descent by returning to the starting position.

The whole workout lasts about 30 minutes. Repeat 3-4 times a week. Perform one series after the other without recovery by climbing, respectively, one repetition and three seconds for resistance exercises and don't skip. *A series of indications and advice on how to keep yourselves active during the epidemic.*

The **pandemic** virus can make it difficult to maintain a physically active lifestyle, but we try with this section to give you some ideas and suggestions.

Based on what we know so far about the new virus, this virus appears to have **very high transmissibility potential**. This is why the ministerial provisions and recommendations are all aimed at avoiding contact with others as much as possible and, if this is necessary, at keeping us at a social distance of at least 1 meter from each other.

These measures obviously have contraindications, and one of these is the difficulty of **carrying out the physical activity**: gyms and fitness centers, as well as city parks, are closed. The traditional *corset* is also *prohibited* unless this takes place in the immediate vicinity of our home. In this period of generalized quarantine, therefore, it is almost inevitable to remain many hours **sitting and inactive**.

What can we do about it?

We start from the indications of the *World Health Organization* (WHO), which even in *normal* times recommends dedicating **at least 20 minutes a day to physical activity**: international guidelines, in fact, identify in 150-300 minutes a week the amount of optimal physical activity to maintain a healthy and correct lifestyle.

Note well that we talk about **lifestyle** in general, precisely because carrying out an adequate and constant physical activity not only affects the much-feared *bacon* but also has countless other benefits for our whole body. Regular physical activity, in addition to making us lose weight by eliminating those extra *pounds*, also helps us to:

Increase **the** body's **immune defenses** and consequently decrease the chances of contracting viruses and diseases

Reduce stress and anxiety, which is a period like the one we are experiencing have certainly increased

Improve sleep quality and consequently our psycho-physical well-being

Once the ideal physical activity *requirement has been* established, we must understand how we can pursue this goal with all the limitations to which we are subject.

The pandemic virus, ten exercises to do to train at home during the quarantine

Among the measures taken by the government to contain the spread of the pandemic virus, there is also the closing of gyms. A piece of news that made the most fanatics of sport and fitness angry and cheered those who in that weight room were obliged to do so by a monthly charge on their checking account. But good news, because in isolation, your home can become the perfect place to continue training or where to start doing it for those who always postpone the fateful registration in the gym until next Monday.

With so much time available, there are many activities that can be done within the home and many exercises to keep you fit despite the appeal of the sofa and the long list of backward TV series. So here is a circuit of ten exercises to continue training in the inexhaustible hours you spend at home. You will need a mat or a common carpet. An elastic band, a sofa, and lots of goodwill.

1. Bend over sofa (10)

Start with the pushups. Just turn your relaxation sofa into useful gym equipment. Place your hands on the sofa so that you have less weight off the arms. Place your hands at a distance from each other equal to the width of your shoulders or slightly wider. Try to go down slowly and touch the sofa with your chest and then return to the starting position, always trying to keep the pelvis retroversion.

2. Elastic Pull (10)

Sitting comfortably on your carpet or mat, take a rubber band and fix it under your feet. If you want to get more tension, spread your feet apart. While adjusting the resistance roll, the elastic in your hand, the more it will be rolled up, the more you will struggle. Pull the elastic towards you with your elbows attached to your body. I recommend shoulders down and straight back, do not arch forward. Then take the elastic back to its original position without ever losing control.

3. Barchetta (30s)

For lovers of fitness and the gym, this is certainly one of the most feared exercises, but also among the most effective for those who want to get a steel abdomen. Classic isometric exercise to train all the abdominal muscles. From a belly up position, we raise the legs and stretch our arms in front of us (simplified version) and hold the position going to form a boat. For the more adventurous, you can bring your arms straight behind the back of the neck. We maintain the position without losing tension or control of the pelvis, which must be reversed for the duration of the exercise.

4. Plank (30s)

Another resistance exercise is highly effective for training the whole body. On your stomach, rest your forearms on the floor in a straight line with your shoulders so that they are parallel to each other. Lift your buttocks, but please, don't keep them too high. I hold the position for 30 seconds. Remember to breathe.

5. Side plank (30s)

Same exercise, but this time goes to strengthen the oblique abs and the transverse muscle of the abdomen. Always free body positions yourself on your side and rest your elbow on the ground and then lift yourself off the floor. The whole-body weight is concentrated on the forearm, which also, in this case, must remain in line with the shoulder.

6. Hyperextensions (30s)

Position yourself lying on the ground with your stomach on the floor (prone position); your legs stretched with your feet hammered. The hands can be placed behind the nape, under the chin, along the sides with the palms of the hand upwards, stretched forward. Hold the position for 30 seconds.

7. Ground bridges (30s)

Lie on your back (belly up), stretch your arms at your sides, bend your knees, rest your feet on the ground and then lift both the buttocks and the pelvis while always maintaining the upper back, shoulders, arms, and head lean on the floor. Raise and hold the position for 30 seconds.

8. Wall chair (30s)

Since all you need for this exercise is a wall, the walls of your home will be perfect. Position your shoulders against the wall, lean your back firmly on it and imagine an imaginary chair. Position your feet at equal distances to your femur from the wall, trying to obtain an angle of approximately 90 degrees. Place your head against the wall and keep your hands at your sides. Hold the position for 30 seconds.

9. Jumping jack (10)

You thought you could get by without cardio? Yes, many parks are closed as well as gyms, but there are exercises at home that can help your aerobic training. Feet united with legs extended and arms at your sides, raise your arms above your head and jump spreading your legs. Always in sync, return to the starting position and continue to repeat the movement without stopping.

10. Elastic stretches (10)

An excellent shoulder exercise is a military press. Standing, pass the elastic under the feet spaced apart shoulder-width apart. Once again, hold the elastic and bring your hands to shoulder height. With your back straight push upwards until your elbow is almost completely extended; check the descent by returning to the starting position.

The whole workout lasts about 30 minutes. Repeat 3-4 times a week. Perform one series after the other without recovery by climbing, respectively, one repetition and three seconds for resistance exercises. And don't cheat.

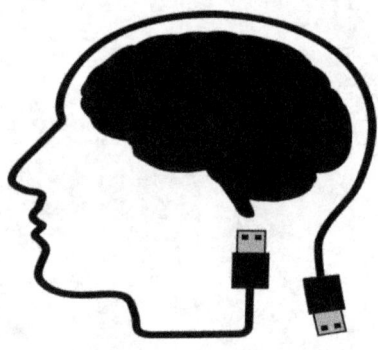

We are facing a new situation for many of us, and as with everything unknown, it generates uncertainty and, above all, fear. Furthermore, when we feel threatened our health and that of our loved ones. No doubt! Our emotional well-being is being affected. But we have to remember that we have overcome other difficulties and that we will also overcome this one. The important thing is to be aware that the **psychological coping** with this situation, generated by the pandemic virus, requires, on our part, an active, adaptive response. The question would be: are we prepared to face it? **Yes, we are!**

We have everything we need, our ability to think, and our emotional resources, skills that we have already used at other times, also difficult. It is true that these circumstances are very novel, and that they have characteristics that radically affect our daily life, in which we feel safe, but our strengths are remarkable, and also, we are not alone, we can and will receive help. In these situations, empathy and solidarity are evident, as well as the enormous involvement of professionals from different areas of our society.

However, in the same way, that there are social groups, such as the elderly, who are more fragile (in this case due to biological reasons) against the pandemic virus, there are people who have a greater **emotional**

vulnerability, people who find this situation It affects them more markedly and they also need more guidance, support, and help.

To these people, who are most emotionally vulnerable, this **Guide to Psychological coping with the pandemic virus** is addressed in the first place. A guide that seeks to identify, reflect, and pay attention to different psychological aspects in this crucial situation.

Emotional Vulnerability and Psychological Coping

Professionals in Psychology would like to see more about **Emotional Health**. The social isolation measures that have been put in place to stop the spread of the pandemic virus significantly affect people's emotional well-being.

We feel uncertainty, fear, and sadness. We go from anguish to laughter, then to worry or guilt. Then, we are surprised by solidarity and joyful hope and back to sadness, which makes our tears flow.

It is natural that this extraordinary situation generates a "roller coaster of emotions," but in general, we are able to "cope with it."

But, just as the pandemic virus affects physical health with greater or lesser intensity depending on biology, there are people who are affected by this situation of isolation and uncertainty much more and have greater difficulty in psychological coping. It is a more vulnerable group, in which we do not always repair; they are people with greater **emotional vulnerability**.

People who have spent years learning how to deal with their hypochondria (currently called disease anxiety), with generalized anxiety problems, with obsessions or obsessive-compulsive disorders, with depressive symptoms. It is not difficult to imagine how the "emergency" measures that have been activated can exacerbate symptoms, if they currently have it, or reactivate symptoms and problems that they have already overcome.

Imagine a person who has managed to stop insistently washing their hands for fear of becoming contaminated or someone who is obsessed with getting sick, how do you think they will feel right now?

It is a time to reflect on our emotions. This does not mean "ruminating" or "not stopping turning around," but rather identifying what we are feeling, knowing how it is affecting us, and acting accordingly, not letting it evolve and worsen.

Like other health professionals, psychologists, and health psychologists, we are committed to providing guidance, techniques, knowledge, and treatment, if necessary, to carry out adequate psychological coping to prevent these difficulties from overflowing us or redirecting the consequences if they are already affecting us.

Take action! Consulting with a psychologist or psychologist can make you implement strategies that allow you to effectively deal with these new situations, identifying and regulating the emotions that occur.

We do not stop hearing that in this stage of social isolation, it is convenient (and it is very true) to maintain the "muscle tone" and therefore do physical exercise. Why not also worry about maintaining a good "emotional tone."

There are also people who have a **high trait of anxiety**, that is, who tend to respond with anxiety to situations of uncertainty. The pandemic virus is affecting the economy of all countries and generating critical situations in companies around the world.

These people with a **high trait of anxiety** could be overwhelmed by the work, economic, and family situation that this pandemic generates.

And let's not forget the people who already lived in isolation prior to this situation. People who were having a hard time getting out of an unwanted solitude and who began, little by little, to carry out social activities outside their home.

Finally, many people, in this new situation that affects them so much psychologically, see how the symptoms and the experience of a previous illness - many times chronic - that they were suffering are aggravated. I'm talking about people with chronic pain, irritable colon, inflammatory bowel disease, cancer.

In a moment like the one we are living, let us attend to this duality of the person: Body and Mind. Let us be aware of our emotions and spend time identifying, understanding, and regulating them. But also, let's empathize with the people who are most emotionally vulnerable, pay them the attention, understanding, and tolerance they may need.

Emotional management in psychological coping

The possibility of our health or that of our loved ones being affected is a natural source of worry and anxiety.

From Psychology, we know the usefulness of all emotions; they are adaptive; they mobilize us and help us to stimulate care and solutions.

In the current circumstances, emotions such as anxiety, fear, sadness, anger, or impatience will be very frequent in most people. These emotions share with each other the function of preserving life and mobilizing ourselves to defend ourselves from what is threatening us - the pandemic virus in this case.

The fear and anxiety help us focus on potential sources of threat or harm.

The uncertainty on how things will evolve on the information we receive, how long the measures will if we are doing well, encourages us to try to recover the perception of control, motivating the search for certainties, imagining possible scenarios, and evaluating the resources we have.

The concern is a cognitive and emotional process that appears to be linked to the above. It has an adaptive function and encourages mental acts such as paying attention to potential negative consequences or anticipating and preparing ourselves to face those possible situations.

The sadness is a normal response to loss assessment. It has the function of assimilating what is happening to us and allows us to reflect on how to deal with the situation.

The fault helps us to become aware of acts and behaviors that have generated damage or risk of harm, both for oneself and for others. It encourages us to repair mistakes and, ultimately, to take responsibility and act accordingly - maintaining isolation and prevention measures, for example.

The anger, has the function to set limits, defend ourselves against threats of harm, and defend our rights.

All these emotions, although unpleasant, fulfill a primary adaptive function, however, when the emotion exceeds levels in intensity and frequency, when it does not respond to a real and objective reason, or overstates the danger, far from helping protection and adaptation. They can contribute to increase the feeling of helplessness and block us in action.

Also, the extraordinary situation we are experiencing puts into play our ability to commit ourselves individually and collectively to a common threat and activates other very relevant and useful, and more pleasant, emotions: **hope, trust, solidarity, empathy, unit, or support**.

In situations like the ones we are experiencing, each person faces circumstances in a very different way, either because of their personal, psychological, or emotional characteristics or because of their beliefs or education, for example, the way in which they understand social relationships or the social commitment.

In this way, many people replace actions aimed at obtaining immediate individual gratification with others that benefit the entire community, making efforts, assuming costs, and rigorously carrying out very uncomfortable measures.

On the other hand, others violate the isolation measures and go out to the street to have fun, or do not maintain distances or safety behaviors.

These differences can generate conflicts between people, feelings of injustice, misunderstanding, guilt, or helplessness.

Emotional management is an essential tool in our life, and it is more so in extraordinary situations like the one we are experiencing.

The key is to learn to identify, understand, and regulate our emotions. And to do so, I would highlight two fundamental strategies.

Two psychological coping strategies for the pandemic virus

1. Adopt a positive problem-solving attitude. The situation we are experiencing is generating - and will generate - many difficulties and problems. It is normal to feel fear, uncertainty, anger, or concern. But we

have to overcome this first stage and prepare to find solutions. Realistically weigh the resources within our reach, focus on what is under our control. Do not anticipate making catastrophic predictions. Adjust expectations about results. Congratulate us on the progress. Collaborate and seek support. In short, focus on solving the problem, adapting to circumstances.

2. Generate, facilitate, and promote pleasant emotions.

In the face of difficulty, pleasant emotions will help us; they will generate greater motivation, stimulation, more resistance to adversity - or resilience.

Enjoying moments of well-being is key to promoting positive attitudes when facing problems, and managing in a more serene and productive way the differences or conflicts with other people or family members, which may arise in moments as delicate as these.

All strategies and activities that enhance and stimulate pleasant emotions are going to be strengths for psychological coping with the pandemic virus.

Psychological coping living alone

It is important that confinement in our homes and the social distance does not become social isolation and feelings of unwanted loneliness.

In the current situation, it makes even more sense to enhance social contact and relationships with friends, family, and coworkers. Use technology to foster these relationships: telephone, video conferences, sharing videos of us and us, letters about how we feel, what worries us, sharing our creations (paintings, drawings, sculptures, video montages, etc.).

Participate in solidarity initiatives that are within our reach. Or carry out leisure or training activities at home connected to groups through videoconferencing or social networks, or sharing the achievements made with friends through social networks. All these shared actions will increase the feeling of belonging and community.

Psychological coping in family

This situation, for many families that have gone from seeing a limited time to being together all day, is supplying a reformulation of the family concept.

We are going to feel and discover new aspects of ourselves, our partner, and our sons and daughters.

We will feel happy with them, but unpleasant and conflicting emotions will also appear, which we could avoid before –by leaving home, for example–, and which we now find ourselves in need to share and face.

Being aware that everything has changed is a fundamental starting point to emotionally manage this new situation.

In this new context, in which we cannot avoid or delay for a long time the resolution of an emotional state, since we are going to be together for many days, three keys will be essential:

· Communication in the couple.

· Empathy.

· The value of emotional regulation in our life.

Family together at home

In these new circumstances, our own family can be a novelty. The daily and habitual activities and obligations: studying, working, playing…, now they are constantly at the side of our partner and our children.

There are no longer differentiated spaces that "free" us from constant interaction and that allowed us, for example, to show our bad mood in a place that does not affect the family. Or allow ourselves emotional states that we usually hide from other people, including our partner and children.

This can be stressful, something that generates anguish, or an opportunity to learn, to show ourselves more natural, just as we are, learning to identify and manage the attitudes or behaviors that can generate discomfort and that before, we simply avoided facing.

It is a well-known and used phrase, so much that it has lost its value, but I can't resist saying that situations like this **are an opportunity**, an opportunity to improve our emotional ties, learn to be more natural and sincere or sincere, to practice empathy and tolerance, to communicate better, to learn more from ours and from us.

But you have to act. A new situation requires new actions, plans, imagination, motivation.

Ideas to stimulate good emotions in family

Make a family planning and hang it in a visible place (the door of the living room, fridge, etc.), which collects the needs, activities of each of the family members, and the joint activities of the whole family and others that enhance coexistence. It will serve to know when someone is working and not interfere; when we can talk or not with friends, depending on whether there is a family "gathering," etc. This is especially useful for children.

For example, everyday mom works from 8 am to 2 pm and dad from 3 pm to 8 pm. At the office; Monday at 12:00 Juan sees his drawings; Tuesday at 20:00 we all cook dinner together at Mario's request, at 16:00 we watch a movie in English with mom, at 12:00 from Monday to Friday 1 hour of dance or sport at home with dad, on Wednesday family debate..., on Sunday special food together to talk about what each one has to do in the coming week.

Reserve spaces and set rules for individual and private moments.

For example: on Wednesdays from 16:00 to 18:00 I need the room for meeting and silence. Every day from 20 to 21, I will be in my room to talk to my partner or friends online and that nobody enters.

Using creativity, stimulating the imagination, brainstorming as a family, let proposals flow that, although at first, they may seem absurd to you, perhaps they can turn into something stimulating (creating a family business for online sales) or fun (propose activities contest with other families).

Establish a family meeting day to review how the family is, to adjust the organization, detect other needs that may have arisen, to have a space to express how each member of the family is.

A new situation with the little ones

The little ones and the little ones need our affection, closeness, calm, patience, and time of exclusive dedication and with the family.

Do not perceive inference despite having to perform other tasks. They need the certainty that we will have moments of the day dedicated to them and that they will be able to express what they feel, that they will be heard, that they will be played with. And above all, that they feel that they are loved, protected, and cared for and that this or any situation will not change that.

To the little ones of the house, it is necessary to explain what this disease is and why they have to be at home to adapt to the new situation. The information we give them has to be simple so that they perceive that at home they are going to be fine.

Let's consider the evolutionary stage in which they are:

· Before the age of 6, they will not know very well why it is necessary to be at home.

· From the age of 7-8 years, they begin to acquire more vocabulary, knowledge of the human body, and understand that they can get sick. They will need more explanations and give them peace of mind.

· At 9-10 years, they already acquire the concept of disease and irreversibility of death. At that age, they will be more aware of the risks of this disease. Give them security.

Useful tips for organizing with the little ones of the house

· Normalize the situation. Explain that we are at home because of the special situation of the whole country, not on vacation. Encourage them to ask you their questions, express their needs and emotions. Set a few times a day so they can do it.

· Let them know that we are going to take advantage of the opportunity to organize and plan school activities, that they will continue learning, but that there will also be time for fun activities, both for them and with the family.

· Set tasks that can be performed. Do not overload them or let them do none. Combine directed activities with free activities.

· If there is more than one boy or girl at home, and they have different ages, they need exclusive time, with brothers and sisters and with family. The smaller they are, the more they will need you.

· Whether you work away from home or at home, tell them the time you will dedicate to your work, and when you will stop to be with them. If you have to leave home, give them the security that you will take care of yourself.

· Maintain some routines similar to the ones they had, combining them with new ones. If there are routines, emotions such as boredom, sadness, stress, or anxiety, which can appear in both parents and children, will be better regulated.

o Sleep rhythms, personal hygiene, meal times.

o Participate in household chores: set the table, clear it, pick up your room, your toys, etc.

o Establish a school homework schedule, to watch movies alone or with the family, or drawings, free play, or set, family activities (board game, cooking, playing hide and seek), physical activity (yoga, dancing).

o Set the time of use of the mobile, tablet, or consoles per week and at the weekend.

Organizing with teenage sons and daughters

The special characteristics of Adolescence can be highlighted in these circumstances. It is important to understand this adolescent stage, empathize with your sons and daughters for the well-being of the whole family.

· **Promote spaces to talk about the situation of change that we are experiencing**. Most teens are in constant contact with information through social media and the internet, but it may not be realistic. It is important to help them understand and correctly interpret the information so that they do not minimize or exaggerate it, leading to inappropriate behaviors.

·   **Give them real and updated information, without alarming them excessively, but without falling into protectionism**. If there is something to which we do not know how to respond, make it normal without lying about it and try to find the answer together. Always convey security and a sense of control, and make it easier for them to ask questions.

·   **Let them express how they feel and normalize fear as adaptive**. It is normal to feel fear and many other emotions, to teach him the good side of feeling them. They may feel scared and helpless and hide it. Others, however, will be alarmed and may even ask questions about catastrophes, the number of deaths, etc.

·   **Help them manage their time and schedules**. It will be more difficult for them to do it themselves. Encouraging daily routines will make them better adapted to the situation until classes resume (study time, homework, or reading at home, collaboration on household chores, etc.). Establish temporal order in your daily behaviors: first do the "obligations" and then the leisure or game activities (computer, video games, etc.).

· **Promote the responsible and limited use of technology,** preventing it from becoming constant and indiscriminate entertainment.

· **Encourage them to be in social contact** with their friends and classmates by video call or by phone, as well as with family members who are away from home.

· **Promote your social awareness**. This is a good time.

26 tips for coping with total pandemic virus quarantine

A list of recommendations to responsibly go through these times of pandemic, prepared by the doctor Sergio Víctor Perrone. Also, detail how long the virus lasts on objects and how to keep up with influenza vaccines

Take care of yourself and others. Think of one to think of all. Decisions during these times of total quarantine in the country and even the world are no longer individual. With the propagation power of the new pandemic virus, what each person does affects the life of the community. For this reason, we present you with a list of 26 "tips" to responsibly go through these times of pandemic and also, specific detail on hygiene and prevention are as follows:

1. All the familiar groups and neighbors known to people with whom it has contact should educate themselves on the subject (adults and children).

2. Accentuate care with people at higher risk (those with previous pathologies) in which any infectious process can aggravate their state of health.

3. Try to ensure that the institutions, buildings, or condominiums where you carry out your activity are interested in the subject and take the appropriate measures for the care of interpersonal contagion.

4. Know the contact number in your city or town to report to if you suspect an infection or violation of the isolation rules instructed by the authorities.

5. Avoid going to nursing homes where or institutions where the entrance of the virus can aggravate the state of health of the guests.

6. Avoid contact with people you don't know.

7. Stay as long as possible in your home. Leave your home only for essential things. Respect the decree of social isolation.

8. If you have a fever, cough, shortness of breath, contact your doctor or health center before attending.

9. Choose a room in the house where you can isolate the one with symptoms or who has proven the pandemic virus infection and separate it from other healthy inhabitants.

10. Cover the mouth when coughing or sneezing using the elbow crease or a disposable tissue

11. Discard the disposable tissue in a safe place (virus permanence on paper can reach 4 days)

12. Wash your hands frequently with soap and water, liquid alcohol, or gel alcohol, especially after coughing, blowing your nose, or sneezing, after using the bathroom, before eating.

13. Clean surfaces and frequently touched objects (tables, handles, switches, telephone, remote controls) daily.

14. If possible, the possible carrier (person with the possibility of being infected) or the infected with or without symptoms (sick) should use a bathroom for their own use; if this is not possible, the possible carrier or the infected person must personally clean the

bathroom after using it (including the door and cupboard handles, taps, toilet, switches).

15. If your home does not have a separate bathroom for the potential carrier or the sick person, the bathroom should be cleaned and disinfected after each time the infected person uses it as much as possible by themselves. In the event that another person must clean the bathroom, they must take all personal isolation measures.

Cleaning and disinfection

16. Wear disposable gloves when handling clothing or objects, clean and / or disinfect material that may have had contact with the virus.

17. Discard gloves after each cleaning.

18. If you use reusable gloves, they should be exclusively dedicated to cleaning surfaces of possible contact with the new virus (to avoid cross-contamination).

19. Wash your hands immediately after removing gloves.

20. If surfaces are dirty, clean them with detergent or soap and water before disinfecting.

Hand washing

21. All members of the household should wash their hands frequently, including after removing gloves and after being in contact with a possible carrier or sick person.

22. Hands should be washed with soap and water for 20 seconds.

23. If you can't use soap and water, use a hand sanitizer that contains at least 60% alcohol

24. Disinfectants are NOT equivalent to washing hands.

25. Avoid touching your eyes, nose, or mouth with after having touched any possibly

contaminated surface (latches, taps, railings, handrails, etc.).

26. It is recommended that you wash your hands especially after: blowing your nose, coughing, or sneezing; After going to the bathroom; before eating or preparing food; after contact with animals or pets; before and after assisting a person in need of care (children, older adults); before and after contacting or handling utensils contaminated or possibly contaminated by an infected or suspected person.

Total pandemic virus quarantine: 25 tips for coping with isolation

The measures have drastically altered the way people conduct their daily lives. But they also provide an opportunity to try new activities and resume those that may have been postponed indefinitely. Here is a list of suggestions to go through this unprecedented period for the vast majority of society

Very recently, close to a billion people are confined around the world as a result of the advance of the pandemic virus. These measures of social isolation, taken with the aim of reducing an amount of contagion that grows exponentially in many countries and approaches 300,000 -with almost 12,000 deaths- ranging from the order to stay home with the exception of essential activities to quarantine absolute.

As an increasing percentage of society enters this unexplored terrain, the question arises of how to cope with an unprecedented amount of time within four walls.

Whether or not you have the possibility of working remotely, the way you spend your free time is inevitably altered. And although this scenario implies the impossibility of carrying out different activities, it also provides the opportunity to try new ones and resume those that perhaps had been postponed indefinitely over the years. All this, with the help of available technology, capable of bringing distances closer and offering practically infinite leisure and learning options.

Here is a list of suggestions to go through this unprecedented period. Museums and virtual artistic functions, applications, podcasts, books, and tutorials are just some of them.

1. Virtual museums

Like other public spaces, museums had to close their doors to prevent crowds from spreading the spread of the pandemic virus. However, many of them - some of the largest in the world included - offer virtual tours for those who wish to consume their exhibitions from quarantine.

Here 10 of them:

Pinacoteca di Brera - Milan; Uffizi Gallery - Florence; Vatican Museum - Rome; Archeological Museum - Athens; Prado - Madrid; Louvre - Paris; British Museum - London; Metropolitan Museum - New York; Hermitage - Saint Petersburg; National Gallery of art – Washington

2. Online tutorials

One of the most popular veins on the internet. Whether on YouTube, social networks such as Instagram or specific websites, the possibility of learning the most diverse crafts and skills is within reach of the keyboard. From software development to drawing to gardening, the alternatives are virtually endless.

3. Try new recipes

The kitchen deserves a special section within the category of tutorials. Entire channels of content have been created for this purpose and are consumed by millions of people on a daily basis. Quarantine presents the opportunity to finally try - ideally with the ingredients that are available to avoid going out unnecessarily - to cook all those dishes whose recipes have been kept over the years, but due to lack of time or will, they were not put into practice. Tasty, Tastemade, Kitchen for All, The Food Network, and Munchies are just a few of them.

4. Listen to new podcasts

The content offering for all audiences has grown exponentially in recent years. Beyond those that focus on the regional and global political and economic situation, podcasts with social, humorous, and general interest content also abound.

The obvious recommendation is the one considered the best of all, regardless of gender: Serial. Narrated by Sarah Koenig, it narrates journalistic investigations throughout multiple episodes. In 2015, it won the Peabody Award for its innovative format and currently holds the record for downloads of any podcast.

5. Play board games

They've probably been gathering dust somewhere in the corner for years. To share the quarantine with other people, this seems like the best opportunity to clean them up and play again. However, the challenge is multiple: in addition to remembering the rules, players must commit to ending without major stressful situations, considering that they have no other alternative to maintaining contact for the near future. For those who are physically alone, many also offer the possibility of playing virtually, either with acquaintances or strangers.

6. Use game apps

In addition to traditional board games, there are numerous virtual gaming applications, and those of trivia usually occupy the first places in the preference rankings. Quiz Up, Trivia Crack, and Kahoot are some of the most popular. While the first two ask predetermined questions from the most diverse categories, the second allows users to create their own games and organizing challenges.

7. Retake contact with affections in distant places

The quarantine physically isolated nearly 1 billion people. But technology has the ability to bring everyone together on the virtual plane, regardless of distance. Therefore, an attractive alternative during confinement may be to re-establish contact with those with whom he separated or lost contact as a result of distance. Applications such as Skype, Zoom, or WebEx allow you to organize individual or group video conferences for free to know what happened to those who were an active part of our lives at another time.

8. Resume the practice of musical instruments

If you have sympathetic neighbors and do so at reasonable times, playing a musical instrument again can be an ideal way to pass the time. Especially if some inhabitant of a nearby building also does it, thus generating the possibility of forming improvised bands. From having instruments on hand but not knowing how to play them, online tutorials abound too. However, such cases will require a higher level of understanding and patience on the part of those closes by.

9. Read

The alternative seems obvious, but it is not less important for that. In addition, different publishers and platforms have decided to release content for free to encourage people to avoid leaving their homes. The application can be downloaded on smart phones, computers, and other devices and provides access to novels, thrillers, essays on feminism, nutrition, biographies, youth sagas, literary criticism texts, and more.

Anagrama, meanwhile, released five titles. The Planeta group has made available a selection of some of the most popular and sold titles to be downloaded for free. Among them is The Shadow of the Wind, by Carlos Ruiz Zafón; The Da Vinci Code, by Dan Brown; The time between seams, by María Dueñas; Men Who Didn't Love Women, by Stieg Larsson and The Chronicles of Narnia:

The Lion, the Witch, and the Wardrobe, by CSLewis. Other writers have done the same with books of his authorship.

At the same time, digital platforms such as Wikisource and others have thousands of books that can be downloaded for free. You can also access the Hispanic Digital Library, the digital archive of the National Library of Spain, for free.

10. Learn the basics of different languages

Learning a language takes time and dedication, factors that can be present during quarantine. Whether through free applications such as Duolingo -which offers the possibility of learning basic aspects of different languages- or virtual classes, the activity can be a rewarding challenge, as well as useful for the personal and professional future.

11. See virtual concerts

The list of musicians who have offered virtual concerts through their social networks increases day by day. Jorge Drexler, Alejandro Sanz, John Legend, Chris Martin of Coldplay, and FitoPáez are just some of the world artists who, for at least a few minutes, helped their fans to pass the time with their iconic songs. Brian May, the guitarist of the historic band Queen, gave his own twist to the interaction with his followers and taught them to play the solo of one of the best-known songs in history: Bohemian Rhapsody Everything indicates that the trend will continue, for what the followers must be attentive to the social networks so as not to lose any advertisement.

12. See virtual plays

Different referents of the theater scene have announced their desire to transmit works virtually. An example is that of Claudio

Tolcachir, who this weekend began to broadcast three works on social networks and already anticipated his intention to put together a program "every day or on weekends." The wind on a violin took place on Friday at 8:00 p.m., while Emilia and Dinamó will do so on Saturday and Sunday at the same time, respectively.

Another alternative is provided by Teatroteca, a Spanish platform for the management and loan of digital content from the Center for Documentation of the Performing Arts (CDAEM), which made more than 1,600 plays and theater shows available. In addition, the New York Metropolitan Opera will broadcast works from its archive for free. Each show starts at 7:30 PM local time (-5 GMT) and is available until 3:30 PM the next day.

13. Do physical exercise

It does not take more than 5 square meters and the body itself to turn any environment into a gym. In addition, online tutorials and applications with exercise routines tailored to the needs and possibilities of users to stay - or get- in shape abound. Some of them, like Instafit or Down Dog, has announced the release of their paid content to contribute from their side during the quarantine.

14. Carry out a thorough cleaning

"To order with Marie Kondo!" It was one of Netflix's most popular shows in 2019. The quarantine allows viewers to channel their guru of inner order and perform the thorough cleanup they've probably been putting off for years and get rid of unnecessary items.

15. Use audiovisual content streaming platforms

Millions of people consume streaming platforms daily. But in times of global pandemics, activity grows exponentially. In this framework, platforms like Movistar plus, such as Amazon, Netflix Acorn TV, offer free subscription plans for a limited time, while DirecTV and Cablevision Flow released some of the premium channels for all their clients. There are also free platforms, such as Mubi, Cine.ar (which offers Argentine cinematographic content), Filminlatino (with Latin American content), and the Internet Archive. And different producers have decided to release part of their content as well. An example in Latin America is that of El Pampero Cine.

16. Write

An activity that may be uncommon for many in normal times but can be rewarding, to make the decision to do it. Fiction, non-fiction, poetry, or simply a diary of the course of the quarantine are possible alternatives for those who consider the possibility of sitting in front of a blank sheet - real or virtual - and leaving their creativity free.

17. Help students

The vast majority of those in the school stage is going through the unprecedented situation of having to attend class virtually, especially primary and secondary students. Those who have the capacity to help them with their tasks are in a key position to make the experience less complex, considering the difficulties that arise from implementing this modality abruptly, perhaps without sufficient infrastructure.

18. DIY

The acronym for Do It Yourself. Sites like Wiki How, Wikipedia for these purposes, offers a comprehensive guide to solving everyday home problems for which perhaps one now has time and, above all, will. It is free and has a Spanish version.

19. Stay updated on the latest news regarding the outbreak

Experts have emphasized time, and again that individual actions play a critical role in containing the spread of the pandemic virus. Therefore, in addition to being quarantined - in the cases indicated- it is key that society is aware of the state of the situation at the local and global level, and is aware of essential public health information to minimize the possibility of contagion own and others. It is also essential to identify and avoid the misinformation circulating about it.

20. Take care of mental health

Mental health is as important as physical health. The exceptional situation that the world is going through, as well as the physical isolation to which a large part of the world population has been subjected, can threaten it. That is why it is essential to recognize the situation and take action to strengthen it. Staying in constant contact with affections and, if you do therapy, continue it virtually, are some examples. To them is also added the possibility of doing yoga or meditating, activities for which there are different applications.

21. Interview older family members

This is an opportunity to record the stories of older family members that we may not remember or do so loosely. Many went through historical periods of society, such as the one we are currently living, and leaving them settled can shape a rich archive, both family and societal.

22. Build playlists

Music accompanies us every day, but it does it even more in times of isolation. Numerous lists of songs alluding to quarantine have already been put together, but time is abundant to create others to suit us, either to go through quarantine or when it is over. All music platforms -Spotify, YouTube Music, Apple Music, among others- provide the possibility of doing it.

23. Brainstorm

English term to refer to the "brainstorm." Alone or with friends, free time is a perfect opportunity to think of ideas that can be innovative, whether on a professional, social, or cultural level.

24. Thank those who continue to work

The quarantine can be cumbersome, but that should not lose sight of the fact that many people continue to work to provide essential services in this extreme time. Health professionals, food and hygiene chain workers, and security personnel are some examples of those who put their health at risk every day of the pandemic. Throughout the world, massive applause has been organized to give due recognition to his work.

25. Make a list of everything you want to do when the quarantine ends

So far, at least, the isolation measures have an end date. And while this does not mean that life will return to how it was before the pandemic began, some of them will be enabled again, probably subject to hygienic restrictions. A list of the activities to be carried out and the affections to visit, always within the framework imposed by the authorities, can give an objective to aspire to once the quarantine is over.

We advise that we should comply with the requirements stipulated by the **World Health Organization**, and we must stay in our homes, so that in this way we can cut the epidemiological chain of the new virus, **protecting** your own health and that of everyone around you.

We hope this book has been able to help providing you the vital information and knowledge you necessarily need to keep check on all the safety measures against the virus.

against the publisher for any reparation, damages, or monetary loss due to the information herein, either directly or indirectly.

Respective authors own all copyrights not held by the publisher.

The information herein is offered for informational purposes solely, and is universal as so. The presentation of the information is without contract or any type of guarantee assurance.

The trademarks that are used are without any consent, and the publication of the trademark is without permission or backing by the trademark owner. All trademarks and brands within this book are for clarifying purposes only and are the owned by the owners themselves, not affiliated with this document.